Cajun Dancing

Cajun Dancing

Ormonde Plater
Cynthia and Rand Speyrer

PELICAN PUBLISHING COMPANY

Gretna 1993

The word "Pelican" and the depiction of a pelican are trademarks of Pelican Publishing Company, Inc., and are registered in the U.S. Patent and Trademark Office.

Library of Congress Cataloging-in-Publication Data

Plater, Ormonde.
    Cajun dancing / Ormonde Plater, Cynthia and Rand
Speyrer.
      p.   cm.
    ISBN 0-88289-970-8
    1. Folk dancing, Cajun.   2. Folk dancing, Cajun—History.
    3. Cajuns—Music.   4. Cajuns—Social life and customs.
    I. Speyrer, Cynthia.   II. Speyrer, Rand.   III. Title.
    GV1624.7.C25P53   1993
    793.3'19763—dc20
                                        92-44203
                                             CIP

Photos by Michael P. Smith

Front cover photo © 1993 by Michael P. Smith, used by permission. Cynthia and Rand Speyrer.

Back cover photo © 1992 by Michael P. Smith, used by permission. From left: Arthur Kastler and Sarah Neher, Maria Amaya and Ormonde Plater, Marie Céleste Robichaux and William Robichaux, Moïse Viator and Alida Viator, Joyce and James Carrington, Cynthia and Rand Speyrer. On fiddle: Gerald Cormier of the Breaux Bridge Playboys.

Manufactured in the United States of America

Published by Pelican Publishing Company, Inc.
1101 Monroe Street, Gretna, Louisiana 70053

To Dewey Balfa (1927–92)

Contents

Preface

Not too long ago, many people in south Louisiana looked down upon Cajun culture. This was partly a result of a difference in language. Most Cajuns of our parents' and grandparents' generation spoke French. Many of them had been raised in families that spoke only Cajun French, and when they started first grade they had to learn to speak English.

In 1921, the legislature made English the official language of Louisiana, and it was compulsory for children to learn English in school. Those who grew up speaking Cajun French at home were urged not to speak it anymore, and they were forbidden to speak it at school. Some of them were even urged to lose their Cajun accents. This pressure to become Americanized resulted in harsh feelings between two elements of south Louisiana society. Many English-speaking Americans looked down upon the French-speaking Cajuns and considered them *basse classe*. Until recently, many people were ashamed to admit that they were of Cajun heritage.

Today the Cajun people have come into the light, and much of their culture is admired and imitated. Their cultural emergence especially includes music and dancing. These forms of artistic expression have existed for generations in south Louisiana, but only now are they attracting favorable attention throughout the world. Cajun music first gained national recognition in 1964 when Dewey Balfa performed with a Cajun trio at the Newport Folk Festival, which also featured folk stars such as Joan Baez and Peter, Paul, and Mary. Dewey and his cohorts, Gladius Thibodeaux and Louis ("Vinesse") LeJeune, were shocked when the crowd of seventeen thousand went crazy with delight. The standing ovation they received profoundly changed Dewey's life and led him to a lifelong career of teaching Cajun music and spreading Cajun culture throughout the world. Before Dewey died in 1992, people from throughout the United States and Canada came to pay a musical tribute to him at the Liberty Theater in Eunice—an event unlike any before.

After Dewey Balfa helped to break the ground for making the Cajuns aware of their heritage, a renewed interest started to take hold in Acadiana. Many young Cajuns began to work diligently to preserve and promote the music, language, and culture.

One of many whom Dewey inspired was Dr. Barry Jean Ancelet, professor of folklore at the University of Southwestern Louisiana.

Dewey's foresight and words of encouragement helped Barry launch the first tribute to Cajun music in 1974, held in the Blackham Coliseum in Lafayette. The concept of this music festival was to have people really *listen* to the music of their heritage. To ensure this outcome, chairs were set up on the coliseum floor, and no provision was made for dancing. The result was a huge success. Those who attended were thrilled with the music, and they left with a feeling of pride and enthusiasm for their culture. Such was the success of this festival that it has grown to become an annual celebration called Festivals Acadiens and is the largest festival of its kind that focuses on Cajun food, music, and culture.

In 1984 two other events helped to make Cajun culture more popular. Paul Prudhomme, a native of Opelousas, blackened a redfish, and soon Cajun cuisine became world-renowned. Instantly, Cajun was *in,* and chefs far and wide set out to reproduce dishes such as seafood gumbo and crawfish étouffée, regional dishes that we so often took for granted.

Another event in 1984 was the Louisiana World's Fair and Exposition in New Orleans. Inside the Louisiana Pavilion and The Back Door, many local people and tourists got their first glimpse of authentic Cajun music and culture. Until then, very few people in New Orleans knew what a Cajun was or were familiar with the area to the west known as Acadiana. The press sent to cover the World's Fair seemed mystified by the rich diversity of this culture. Many in the media were so moved by the music they heard and the food they ate that they set out to Acadiana to investigate the region. During the next few years, feature stories on Mulate's in Breaux Bridge, Fred's Lounge in Mamou, Marc Savoy's Music Center in Eunice, and many other bastions of Cajun culture appeared on national television and in major magazines and newspapers throughout the world.

The traditional *courir du Mardi Gras,* or Mardi Gras run, celebrated in the small, rural community of Mamou was covered not only by our national press but by a Japanese film crew. The event was even featured in detail in a front-page article in the *Wall Street Journal.* While the extensive coverage seemed to open the doors for many Cajuns to reclaim their cultural heritage with a sense of pride, sometimes the coverage painted false stereotypes. Much of this fakery is the result of tremendous commercial efforts to Cajunize everything from alligator to zucchini.

Now that Cajun life has become popular, it is imperative to reveal the Cajun people as they really are. Many Cajuns have worked hard to improve themselves, educationally and financially. Today the Cajuns you are most likely to find are not barefoot fur trappers but doctors, bankers, farmers, teachers, storekeepers, nurses, accountants, and other respected members of the community. While *joie de vivre* seems to be the Cajuns' hallmark, they are not clones of Justin Wilson.

Cajun music and dance will continue to be celebrated as they have been for generations in south Louisiana, but now it is up to us to nurture the Cajun culture handed down by our forebears and share it with the world. While it is vitally important to preserve and promote the culture, it must be allowed to grow. One cannot live forever in the past. As Dewey Balfa said repeatedly, unless Cajun music continues to change, it will die. We must draw from the past, he said, but we must also allow our culture to breathe so that it remains alive and gives birth to new and even better traditions. As with any art form, there is an inherent dynamic quality, which insists that the form be permitted to change. One cannot preserve the music, dance, or any other aspect of a culture in a vacuum for posterity. While it is important to keep the dance traditions of the past, we must also reflect the dance customs of today, which will become the traditions of tomorrow.

It is with our love for the Cajun people and culture that we present to you the Cajun dance of south Louisiana. Our hope is that you will enjoy the dancing as much as we have. We hope that you share the dance steps you learn with others, just as our families shared their love of music and dance with us. Thus, the Cajun dance traditions we know will continue to grow and survive.

Acknowledgments

This book includes 270 photographs of dance steps, taken by Michael P. Smith, who has spent much of his life documenting the cultural scene in south Louisiana. In these pictures, Cynthia and Rand Speyrer perform the waltz, two-step, and Cajun jitterbug; Sarah M. Neher joins them in the troika and two-couple routine, and Irvin P. Pelegrin in the two-couple routine.

Many others contributed to this project. We especially thank:

René Babineau, Catherine Brookshire Blanchet, Floyd Soileau, Floyd Sonnier, Diana C. Polizo-Schlesinger, Patricia K. Rickels, and Steve Winn, for their help, information, and suggestions.

Susanne Baber and the New Orleans Athletic Club, and Lynn Boutin and Mulate's of New Orleans, for lending their facilities.

Laurie and Edith McKeown, our hosts in the fishing village of Chéticamp on Cape Breton Island, Nova Scotia, for providing us with an evening of Acadian music, and Edith for dancing *la gigue*.

How to Use This Book

This book may be used alone or with two videotapes produced in 1993 by Cynthia and Rand Speyrer. The first is *Introduction to Cajun Dance* and the second is *Advanced Cajun Dancing*. Both are distributed by Pelican Publishing Company and sold either separately or with this book.

Cajun Dancing

Laissez les bons temps rouler *by Floyd Sonnier, Beau Cajun Art Gallery and Studio, Scott, Louisiana. Copyright 1992 by Floyd Sonnier. Used by permission.*

A World of Dance

J'ai été-z-au bal hier au soir,
j'va revenir encore à soir.
Si l'occasion se présente,
j'va retourner demain au soir.

I went to the dance last night,
I'll come back again tonight.
If the occasion presents itself,
I'll return tomorrow night.

—From "J'ai été-z-au bal," a two-step dance tune played
by Iry LeJeune and many others.

Dancing belongs to the language of a people. It is a way of speaking through rhythm, movement, and feeling. It reflects the vitality of a people, their sensitivity, poise, and artistry. It reveals their liveliness and sense of fun. It speaks of their need to reach out to others, touch, and hold on. It issues a powerful invitation to join them and celebrate with them. The Cajun people of south Louisiana are rich in this mode of expression.

The world of the Cajuns is partly geographical. The triangular country in which Cajuns have spread and become concentrated is commonly known as Acadiana. Its southern border is the coast of the Gulf of Mexico from Barataria Bay in the east to the Sabine River in the west. In the east, the country extends north to the outskirts of New Orleans. It passes along the east bank of the Mississippi River, crosses to the west bank just below Baton Rouge, and continues through Pointe Coupée Parish to its northern point in Avoyelles Parish. In the west, the country slopes down to connect with the Texas border near Lake Charles.

Acadiana embraces three long bayous, Lafourche, Terrebonne, and Teche, the vast marshlands west of the river delta, the great swamp of the Atchafalaya River basin, and the flat prairies of southwest Louisiana. It includes the border territory around Port Arthur and Beaumont, called Lapland because Cajuns lap over into east Texas. It also spills over into two big cities, New Orleans and Baton Rouge, where many Cajuns have settled as a substantial minority.

But the Cajun world is also social and cultural, a way of life centered on large and closely knit families, strongly attached to their homes, their land, their communities, and the Catholic faith. It is a world of heritage, assimilation, and inclusion. According to an old saying, one becomes *'cadien* or Cajun "by the blood, by the ring, and by the back door."[1] That is, a Cajun is someone either descended from an original Acadian from Nova Scotia who settled in Louisiana, married into a Cajun family, or absorbed by choice into Cajun culture.[2]

Dancing has always been a vital part of this cultural group. In the Cajun country of Louisiana, anyone looking for a dance has no trouble finding one. Anyone looking for someone to dance with has no trouble finding a partner. Cajuns dance in their homes and yards, in dance halls, restaurants, bars, and lounges, in church and school halls, in parks and streets, at fairs and festivals. They dance whenever *l'occasion se présente*.

Bals de maison **and** Salles de danse

From colonial days until the 1930s, it was the custom among the Cajuns to hold a *bal de maison* or house dance on Saturday night.[3] The French naturalist C. C. Robin, touring Louisiana in 1804, described an early *bal* in an Acadian community up the river from New Orleans:

> Everyone dances, even *Grandmère* and *Grandpère* no matter what the difficulties they must bear. There may be only a couple of fiddles to play for the crowd, there may be only four candles for light, placed on wooden arms attached to the wall; nothing but wooden benches to sit on, and only exceptionally a few bottles of *Tafia* diluted with water for refreshment. No matter, everyone dances. But always everyone has a helping of *Gumbo*, the Creole dish *par excellence*; then "Good Night," "Good Evening," "So Long," "See you next week" (if it isn't sooner).[4]

For more than a hundred years, this scene was replayed every Saturday night throughout the region where Acadians had settled.

The weekly dance was a social event of great importance, gathering the people of a community at one of their homes. They came to visit each other, celebrate their joy in life, and, among the unmarried, court a sweetheart.

Families served as host on a rotating basis. As the weekend approached, news of the location spread quickly. In the prairie country of southwest Louisiana, messengers on horseback galloped from house to house, holding a red handkerchief on a stick, which they tied to the gate of the house where the dance was to be held. Along Bayou Lafourche, where houses were closely packed, neighbors shouted the news from porch to porch. Later, in some places, invitations were announced at mass the Sunday before.

The host family cleared the furniture from the front two rooms of the house, placed chairs and benches along the walls, and hung kerosene lanterns in every room and the yard. Often the weather was hot, and the crowd was expected to spill outside.

Men and women arrived on foot or hitched their horses and buggies to the fence. In the early years they came barefoot in coarse, everyday dress; later they wore their best clothes, including shoes (which they seldom wore at other times). Mothers sent young children to bed in another room, known as *le parc aux petits*. They sometimes had to go into this room and nurse crying infants. Impatient to get back and worried about the husbands they had left on the dance floor, they hushed the babies, telling them *"fais do-do,"* baby-talk for "go to sleep." The phrase caught on, and *fais do-do* came to mean any public Cajun dance.[5]

Almost everyone, young and old, was eager to dance every dance, with many different partners, but there were social limits. Fighting and other rowdy behavior were forbidden (not always with success), and courtship was strictly controlled. When not dancing, young couples were allowed to talk but not to hold hands. Mothers watched their unmarried daughters carefully to see that they did not touch bodies with their partners as they danced. They warned each girl to put her left hand on the boy's shoulder to keep him at a safe distance. A single girl was never permitted to leave the dance alone or with a boy.

The musicians also came from the neighborhood. Usually a hat was passed to collect money for the fiddlers and other musicians, who earned a dollar or two apiece. In the early days the fiddle was the reigning instrument, and usually two fiddlers played in harmony. (As late as the 1980s, Dennis McGee and Sady Courville played twin fiddles in the old style.) They played by ear, from memory. In the European tradition, most dances are accompanied by instrumental music, but Cajun musicians made up lyrics to sing with the dance tunes. Someone beat the rhythm with metal spoons or a steel triangle called a *'tit fer* or little iron.

The noise of the dancers often drowned out the music. The musicians frequently had to place their chairs on a table to be seen and heard by the crowd. The fiddlers scraped hard with their bows and sang in high, screeching voices, a style that continues to this day among some musicians. In the 1880s German merchants began importing the diatonic accordion, a loud, squawking instrument that soon became an essential part of the band. It eventually dominated the music, especially after its quality improved in the 1920s.

With occasional breaks for eating and drinking, men and women danced both traditional dances and the popular steps of the day. Many of these were derived from European dances. In the nineteenth century, settlers and travelers in the region, spreading through the major towns and along the waterways, continuously expanded the Cajun repertoire with the latest dances from Paris, London, and other cultural centers.

A hundred or more years ago, Cajuns knew far more steps than they do today. They danced the new waltzes, polkas, mazurkas, and varsoviennes. They were especially fond of fast *valses à deux temps* (waltzes in double time), in which couples whirled about the floor at a dizzying pace. Groups of six, eight, or more couples filled the floor for *cotillons,* contredanses, reels, and various other longway and circle dances. Among the most popular group dances were quadrilles, square dances in which four couples to each set danced graceful figures to five different pieces of music. Pairs or groups competed in the noisy, rapid shuffling of jigs and breakdowns. Among the more curious steps, as Dennis McGee recalled years later, were handkerchief dances and a dance called Jim Crow, in which men and women jumped together from side to side "like a toad."[6]

Also popular were new dances for couples, with not only European but also African, Caribbean, and American Indian roots. These included the two-step and its simpler cousin, the one-step. One dance to two-step music was called the jilliling, after the soprano Jenny Lind.[7] By the early years of the twentieth century, most of the old dances and steps had started to go out of style. Eventually, only the waltz and the two-step remained in fashion.

The crowd in the house was often too large for everyone to dance at the same time, and some had to wait their turn outside. The host controlled who could come inside and dance, and who had to step outside in rotation. If the weather permitted, those outside danced on the dirt and grass and sometimes on boards laid in the yard. In some places the dancing went on past midnight, even to dawn, when the dancers dispersed to go to mass. Sometimes a member of the band had to take drastic steps to end the dance, stepping outside, firing a pistol in the air, and calling out, "*Le bal est fini!*"

The dances on Saturday night went on almost all year round. In Lent, however, Catholic priests discouraged these dances, and devout parents did not allow young couples to dance to instrumental music. As a substitute, Cajuns used one of their oldest forms of entertainment, *les danses rondes,* which emphasized dancing by a group rather than by couples. Neighborhood groups gathered on Sunday at one of their homes for dances in the shape of a circle, often around an old oak tree. These circle dances were known as *les soirées de carême,* or lenten evening parties. Actually, the parties started after mass in the morning and lasted until midnight. They attracted as many as a hundred persons, from the very young to the very old and especially those of marrying age, all of whom came and went during the day. The lenten circle dances were common until the early 1930s, about the same time as public dance halls began to replace the old house dances.

Starting in the late nineteenth century, Cajuns began to build *salles de danse* or dance halls to accommodate the weekly *fais do-do*. At first, these halls were family or neighborhood structures, houses with one large front room instead of two small ones. Later, the dance halls resembled large country stores and were designed as the cultural centers of neighborhoods, villages, and towns. Some were community *pavillons,* and some were halls owned by individuals. Although Cajuns continued to hold *bals de maison* in their homes, by the 1930s much of their social life took place in these free-standing halls. They came by foot, on horseback, and in buggies, wagons, and cars. With the arrival of automobiles, trucks, and busses in the 1920s, and better roads in the 1930s, it became possible for family and neighborhood groups to travel many miles to a dance hall.

The typical hall was a large and ramshackle building. Across the front stretched a dance floor, always crowded, with benches or bleachers around the sides for the girls with their mothers, other

La cage aux chiens *(the dog yard) in a dance hall near Crowley, 1938.* (Photo by Russell Lee, Farm Securities Administration collection, Library of Congress)

A Saturday night fais do-do *in south Louisiana, 1945*. (Photo by Elemore M. Morgan, The Historic New Orleans Collection, Acc. No. 1976.139.127)

women, and married men. The unmarried men stood in a fenced-off area known as *la cage aux chiens* or dog yard, from which they emerged between dances to seek a partner. Refreshments were sold in a booth or connecting room. In the back was a room for the babies, and in another room men played a fast-moving, dangerous card game called *bourré*. During Prohibition, men also hid bottles of moonshine all over the place, in buggies, wagons, and cars, and under the dance hall, and came out for a drink between dances.

The men paid a fee of ten, fifteen, or twenty-five cents, depending on the local economy. They paid to dance, not to listen. Unmarried boys and girls always went to the dance separately. Girls were still chaperoned by their mothers, a custom that continued into the 1940s. *Les veuves*, the widows, often sat as a group and expected every man to dance with them. The musicians sat on a platform, sometimes with chicken wire in front so that no one could throw pop bottles or trash at them. There were few windows, ventilation was poor (despite one or two big fans), and the dancers quickly worked up a sweat. One event of the evening was *la danse pour le gâteau*, a contest in which dancers were eliminated until the last couple won a cake.

In an interview with Ann Allen Savoy, the fiddler Dewey Balfa described a typical dance hall of the 1940s and 1950s:

> Imagine that you're walking into this big building. Ninety per cent of the time you could see the rafters. Along the walls there were benches, sometimes two, sometimes three levels high, like you would have in school. The mothers would escort their daughters to the dance halls and they would bring along their little children and they would sit there on those bleachers as long as the dance went on. As you walked in, there was a fence with a gate where you could come in and watch the people dance and listen to the music if you didn't have any money to go into the dance hall.[8]

Most dances at the local hall lasted only a few hours. Sometimes they assumed the length of a marathon. In a few places, the dances lasted all Saturday night, broke up at dawn for early mass, and after a few hours' sleep resumed Sunday afternoon for another session lasting until midnight. As late as the 1950s, a dusk-to-dawn dance was held every week at the pavilion on Grand Isle. Three local musicians played the accordion, fiddle, and triangle, and the hall included a *parc aux petits*. The Grand Isle *fais do-do* carried on a tradition of all-night dancing observed in 1893 at nearby Chênière Caminada, just before that island community was destroyed in a hurricane.[9]

With the rise of the dance halls, musicians began to organize bands, composed of those who had learned their craft at the *bals de maison*. These groups were amateur, as Cajun bands largely remain today: men who worked as farmers, fishermen, carpenters, schoolteachers. (Women rarely played, although this has begun to change.) Each held a regular job and played one or more dances a week, four strenuous hours a dance—or longer, for dances lasting until dawn. The dance halls paid them maybe four or five dollars apiece. During the Great Depression in the 1930s, and even later, when people came to dance but didn't have enough money to enter the hall, the musicians got about half the money paid at the door. Some of them, like the accordionist Iry LeJeune in the 1940s and early 1950s, carried their instruments in flour sacks and hitched rides to and from dances.

At first, dance-hall bands included the fiddle, accordion, and triangle; later, guitars, drums, and amplified instruments were added. Because of the din of the crowd and the roar of the electric fans, the musicians stood to play, and they used microphones and put electric amplifiers (often hooked to car batteries with engines running) on their instruments to make them louder. Some musicians today prefer to play in the old manner, seated, and a few even play without an amplifier.

Dennis McGee, born in 1893, recalled the evolution of dances during his youth: "When I was growing up, people danced to reels. They stopped dancing reels when I was young. They continued to dance contredanses throughout my courting days."[10]

After the 1920s, the waltz and the two-step emerged as the major dances. Dance styles evolved to suit the crowded space and larger number of dancers. To one old-timer, "dancing well meant dancing together in unison with little motion of the upper body."[11] This does not mean that Cajuns are lifeless on the dance floor. Cajuns like to dance fast. Couples in their eighties and nineties often treat the waltz like a quarter-horse race, leaving slower dancers in the dust as they fly around the course. The two-step is no less athletic. Guitarist Joe Barry comments:

> With the two-step the Cajuns like to hit the floor. They're notorious with their left hand, they hug tight with the right, and their left hand is like a swinging ball. And they turn fast and do that two-step and they like to *hit* the floor![12]

During the Second World War and the decades thereafter, young Cajuns adopted another fast step with swinging moves, the six-count dance called the swing or jitterbug. Gradually they invented steps, borrowed moves from here and there, added figures from older dances, mixed everything with graceful movement, and gave the dance a distinctive look and cultural flavor.

Another distinct group in Acadiana is the Creoles, who have close ties of culture and blood to their Cajun neighbors. In south Louisiana, a Creole (from the Portuguese *crioulo,* an African slave born in the New World) is a native-born descendant of African, French, or Spanish ancestors. From colonial times until today, a person of African descent and French heritage (and often French blood) has been called variously *nègre créole,* black Creole, or simply Creole. Generally today, blacks of French heritage prefer Creole.[13]

The Creoles also have a long tradition of dancing. In colonial Louisiana, during the eighteenth century, African slaves held parties and *bals* in their quarters, and free people of African descent organized dances attended by large numbers of slaves and even poor whites.[14] In the nineteenth century, the open partying of the Creoles in rural areas evolved into *bals de maison* on Saturday night.

By the middle of the twentieth century, the older style of music at these house dances was little different from Cajun music. It used the same instruments and same songs. Today it is dying out, with only older persons attending the dances. A few old musicians carry on the tradition: Bois-Sec Ardoin, Canray Fontenot, and the Carrière brothers.

Younger black musicians developed their own style of music, originally called *la-la* or *juré* and later zydeco. The word *zydeco* (or *zarico*, a more accurate pronunciation) comes from the first two words of an expression among Louisiana blacks: "*les haricots sont pas salés*" or "the snap beans are not salty." (When times are hard, poor people can't afford salt pork for seasoning.) The expression became the title of a song made popular by the great zydeco musician Clifton Chenier in the 1950s. The term *zydeco* also refers to a dance event, as in, "Let's go to the zydeco."

In the older zydeco dance halls, centered in the Opelousas region and scattered elsewhere in the Cajun heartland, the music remains traditional, mixing Cajun sounds and French lyrics with African and Caribbean rhythms. This style, played by musicians such as Boozoo Chavis and John Delafose, appeals mainly to the Creoles but is also gaining wide popularity outside of Louisiana.

There is also a progressive style of zydeco, played in newer halls in the Lafayette area and other cities. This style is "jazz, blues, and rhythm and blues mixed with French,"[15] fast and with lyrics in French or English or both, but mainly in English. Played by musicians such as C. J. Chenier, Terrance Simien, Buckwheat Zydeco, and Rockin' Dopsie, and by Queen Ida in California, the progressive style has introduced zydeco to the rest of the world.

Zydeco bands usually include either a piano accordion or a double-row or triple-row diatonic accordion, electric guitar, and a *frottoir* or corrugated steel rubboard shaped to fit over the shoulders and chest. The *frottoir* is descended from the washboard, which early Creoles rubbed with metal spoons or bottle openers. (Some Cajun bands also use a *frottoir*.) The progressive bands add a wind instrument such as the saxophone. Older Creoles dance the old-style waltzes and two-steps and also use a subdued style of zydeco dancing. Younger Creoles use faster steps and other moves distinctively their own. Zydeco music and dancing have become important in Louisiana culture, and many young Cajuns have also learned the Creole dance steps.

Fais do-dos and **Honky-Tonks**

Today Cajuns and Creoles go dancing in many places. Dozens of dance halls can be found throughout south Louisiana.[16] Places with Cajun music and dancing are especially thick in the heartland of the region, Breaux Bridge, Lafayette and its suburbs, Opelousas, Eunice, Mamou, and the towns and villages scattered among them. Drivers on the weekend sometimes see signs announcing "Fais Do-Do" or "French Dance Tonite." More often only the sound of a fiddle or accordion, with a cluster of cars outside, reveals the dance.

A few places are the old-style, freestanding halls, with a bar along one wall or in a separate area, space for the band at one end, and tables and chairs along the sides of the dance floor. The old custom was to sprinkle cornmeal for smooth dancing; many places still do this. Most of the older halls are open for dancing only one or two nights a week, but in each community they attract a loyal following, which keeps the place in business.

The cathedral of *salles de danse* is La Poussière in Breaux Bridge. Years ago, when the hall had a dirt floor, customers gave it a French nickname meaning "the dust." The present wood floor is large, smooth, and waxed. Walter Mouton and the Scott Playboys have been the house band for about thirty years. Little has changed over the years, and many of the patrons are Cajun-speaking local people who frequent the hall every Saturday night.

Harry's Club is another Breaux Bridge favorite for local dancers. On Sunday evenings this place is packed with many of the same people who were at La Poussière the night before. Even more rustic and casual is Kaiser's Place, a wooden honky-tonk that rarely sees a tourist at its Friday night dances.

North of Eunice, on the road to Mamou, is another famous old dance hall, the Lakeview Club, part of an aging campground nestled in trees. The Lakeview, Bourque's and Guidry's in Lewisburg, and Snook's in Ville Platte belong to a generation of old halls dating from the 1940s and 1950s. They are social centers in their small communities. Following a venerable custom, many of them allow anyone to come inside but charge a fee to enter the dance area. They attract mainly older people who prefer the traditional waltz and two-step.

Sometimes it is hard to distinguish between a dance hall and a honky-tonk. Most dance halls have a bar at one end or in an adjoining room with connecting windows, where patrons can drink and watch the dancing. The term honky-tonk loosely covers bars, lounges, taverns, and beer halls, where drinking beer, meeting old friends, and talking Cajun French are the main business. Many of these places have dance floors, sometimes large, more often small, and Cajun or zydeco bands play one or two nights a week. D. L. Menard's famous song "La porte d'en arrière" begins:

> *Moi et la belle on avait été-z-au bal,*
> *on a passé dans tous les honky-tonks.*[17]

> Me and my girl had gone to the dance,
> we passed inside all the honky-tonks.

Menard may have had in mind a place like Smiley's Bayou Club in his hometown of Erath. When strangers enter the dark hole of Smiley's, patrons turn to stare. To speak Cajun French is to be one of them; to dance Cajun (only the waltz and two-step) is almost as good. According to a sign above the bandstand, no one under eighteen is allowed, and you may not dance "A. with shorts, B. same sex." A sign in Fred's Lounge in Mamou, honky-tonk of honky-tonks, warns: "This is not a dance hall. If you get hurt dancing, we are not responsible."

At the other end of the social spectrum is the Liberty Theater, a famous old movie house in Eunice. In recent years the Liberty has become the setting for a Saturday night radio program called "Rendez Vous des Cajuns," in the rustic style of the Grand Ole Opry or Louisiana Hayride about fifty years ago. The musicians play on stage. Two rows of seats have been removed up front for the old-timers, children, and others who want to dance. During breaks, a woman in a *garde-soleil* or sunbonnet gives a recipe or a humorist tells a joke. Seated on the left, host Barry Jean Ancelet carries on a lighthearted commentary in Cajun French, with a little English thrown in for the tourists, and occasionally hops down to sprinkle cornmeal on the sloping dance floor. At this family gathering, liquor is not served.

Zydeco dance halls are another genre entirely. They exist mainly in the heartland of Acadiana, around Opelousas and Lafayette. The most famous is Slim's Y Ki Ki, a few miles north of Opelousas, which has a dance every Saturday night and every other Friday. While zydeco halls are primarily for Creoles, Cajuns and other whites are welcome so long as they follow the local customs. Those who enter traditional zydeco halls such as Slim's, Richard's in Lawtell, and Gilton's in Eunice and start to dance Cajun (circling the floor) may receive a polite suggestion to dance zydeco (not circling).

On any weekend, fans can usually track down their favorite zydeco stars: Boozoo Chavis is likely to take the stand at Gilton's, Ann Goodly at Papa Paul's in Mamou (Paul Fontenot is her grandfather), and Nathan Williams at El Sid O's (owned by his brother Sidney) in Lafayette. These and other zydeco halls generally keep late hours, starting at nine or ten in the evening. Many zydeco halls are in remote sections of town or way out in the country, with cattle for neighbors, without a phone and often without a sign, and hold dances as the spirit moves. Like their erratic schedules, their reputation spreads by word of mouth.

In the last twenty years, combination restaurants and dance halls have extended throughout the region. The most famous of these is Mulate's in Breaux Bridge, which has branches in Baton Rouge and New Orleans. Other leading restaurant-dance halls are Randol's in Lafayette, Préjean's in nearby Carencro, Bélizaire's in Crowley, and Michaul's in New Orleans. These halls have attracted a new generation of Cajun musicians with higher pay, and they provide a family atmosphere where children and young adults can learn to dance. Most of them furnish a band every night of the week. In some of the halls, the management offers free dance lessons. Many other restaurants through Cajun country hire a band one or two nights a week.

In all the dance halls, honky-tonks, and restaurants, people come to dance but also to socialize. In places that allow children, families come together, and children dance with adults and each other. Many other dancers are adult couples whose children have grown up and left home. Dance halls also have become increasingly popular with the younger generation. In the big cities, divorced and other single women sometimes ask men to dance with them. Throughout the region, both men and women take great pleasure in guiding a guest through a waltz or two-step.

Serious dancers in Acadiana are likely to move from place to place, starting Friday night and ending Sunday night, as they make the rounds of dance halls, restaurants, honky-tonks, church parish halls, and local fairs and festivals.

The Eunice and Mamou area is typical. Every Saturday morning, Fred's Lounge in Mamou is jammed with local people and tourists from all over the world. They dance on a barroom floor powdered with cornmeal, listen to the band in their midst, and constitute the jostling, beer-drinking audience in a radio program broadcast in Cajun French. The hostess, Tante Sue, welcomes guests, serves beer and boudin, and makes them feel at home. When Fred's winds down in the early afternoon, the local crowd moves two doors to Diana's Brass Rail or down the road to another lounge north of Eunice. In the evening, there is the show at the Liberty Theater, and some of the same people end up at the Lakeview Club or the VFW hall in Eunice. On Sunday afternoon, they may go to a dance at one of the civic clubs, lodges, church halls, or school gyms in the area.

In the big cities every weekend, customers pack the dance halls, restaurants, and nightclubs with Cajun music. Lafayette, regarded as the cultural capital of Acadiana, offers a wide range of Cajun and zydeco dance spots. On Friday evenings in the fall and spring, young people throng Jefferson Street in the old section of town for a popular street dance called "Downtown Alive!" The dance is sometimes Cajun, sometimes zydeco, sometimes something else. Afterwards, and on Saturday night, many of them head for dances at El Sid O's Club, Grant Street Dance Hall, Hamilton's Place, and Maison Creole. Randol's and Préjean's draw family crowds for dinner and dancing. Both tourists and local people visit Vermilionville, a theme park recreating a bayou settlement, which has a Cajun dance every afternoon in a hall resembling an old cotton mill.

In the New Orleans area, dancers pick among several floors. Tipitina's, one of the most famous music halls in the country, sets aside Sunday evening for a lively *fais do-do* attended by a mostly single crowd, who inspire Bruce Daigrepont to play fast waltzes and two-steps with a complicated rhythm along with traditional Cajun music. Another group of dancers shows up at Mulate's on Wednesday and Friday nights. Across the river in Westwego, the Firemen's Hall has a dance every week or so, usually on Sunday afternoon, on a large floor resembling an old-time dance hall in the country. (For a list of places to dance in south Louisiana and east Texas, see Appendix A.)

With few exceptions, every festival in south Louisiana features Cajun or zydeco music. These events range widely in size and importance, from the ten-day Jazz and Heritage Festival in New Orleans, to local festivals honoring some aspect of culture, to church and school fairs. Most festivals draw large numbers of people and offer many opportunities for dancing.

At the big festivals in New Orleans, Lafayette, and elsewhere, crowds fill the open spaces in front of bandstands to dance on the grass and dirt. The major Cajun celebration is the huge Festivals Acadiens in Lafayette, a multifestival event in mid-September including the Festival de Musique Acadienne, where the dancers raise clouds of dust; when it rains, they slosh and slide barefoot and twirl in the mud. On the Saturday before Labor Day, crowds descend on a hot, treeless field in Plaisance, north of Opelousas, for the Southwest Louisiana Zydeco Music Festival, featuring many big-name bands. At the smaller festivals and fairs, often a band will perform in a tent or hall or in the yard, surrounded by local people in rows of folding chairs. Sometimes there is even a plywood dance floor. (For a list of fairs, festivals, and events, see Appendix B.)

Cajun dancing has several eager promoters. They include scholars at the University of Southwestern Louisiana in Lafayette, dance instructors in almost every town, and fans everywhere. The Cajun French

Waltzing in the mud at the Festival de Musique Acadienne in Lafayette, 1992. (Photo by Ormonde Plater)

Music Association (CFMA) has chapters in New Orleans, Baton Rouge, Houma and the bayou country, Lafayette, Eunice and the prairie country, Lake Charles, Port Arthur and the east Texas country, and Houston. The CFMA sponsors several festivals and dance competitions, including a big awards festival in Lafayette on the weekend in mid-August.

In homes and yards, and in the street, groups of people get together for dances, even though recorded music often replaces the live bands of the old *bals de maison*. Nearly every barbecue, shrimp, crawfish, and crab boil, family reunion, neighborhood party, or other celebration offers an occasion to dance.

Raymond E. François, a fiddler who grew up near Eunice, describes the social aspect of Cajun dancing, rooted in love of family and friends, as it was in the past and is today:

> For us, dancing was an important social activity. It's not just for dating or married couples. Couples do attend dances together, but they probably don't dance exclusively with each other. Family groups often attend together, and it's not unusual to see a grandson waltzing with his grandmother. And it's all right to ask someone you don't know to dance, although your invitation isn't always accepted.[18]

Sometimes large numbers of dancers take the floor as a unit, in modern versions of old group dances. The zydeco train, a chain dance done by some Cajun dancers in a few places, probably reflects the influence of the second-line tradition in New Orleans. While the band plays a rollicking two-step melody sounding like a choochoo, the shuffling dancers form a long line that snakes around the floor, crosses itself, and shrinks and expands in a rolling circle.

Another group dance, the Cajun freeze, is derived from a country-western line dance. Danced without partners, it gives unescorted women a chance on the floor. All the dancers face the same direction and move in unison, two steps right, two left, two back, then rocking forward twice and turning to the left; they repeat this over and over until the music ends.

Dances often include party games and other social customs. As in the old days, contests sometimes involve the elimination of dancers. In the potato dance, each couple holds a potato between their foreheads and, with hands behind backs, dances the waltz and two-step. The couple lasting the longest without dropping the potato wins a prize.

Other customs pertain to the entire event. One old convention still found in south Louisiana is *le bal de noce*, or wedding dance, often held in a dance hall. In the old days when people were poor, the owner paid the wedding couple ten or fifteen dollars to have the dance at his hall, and charged fifteen cents' entrance fee. Today the couple usually rents the hall. During the first song, "La marche des mariés" (wedding march), the newlyweds link arms and, followed by the wedding party, walk around the dance floor at least twice. Then they dance the first waltz. Afterwards all dance, and every man present is expected to dance with the bride and pin money on her veil.[19]

During the carnival season just before Lent, dancing takes place all across the Cajun landscape. The owner of a country dance hall may ask a group of masked riders, or "Mardi Gras" as they are known, to entertain the customers. They rush into the hall, dance together, and start dancing with the customers. The captain follows with a whip. He chases the revelers under tables, where they tease the women into mock fright and outrage, and finally corners them howling in the center of the dance floor. There they chant a Mardi Gras song, beating on the floor with their hands.[20]

Throughout Cajun country, dancing remains a vital part of life. Following the social custom of their ancestors for many generations, men and women and sometimes whole families go out to dance once or twice a week. As young people learn from their elders and each other, and others discover the enjoyment of the waltz, two-step, and Cajun jitterbug, the dances of the Cajuns are passed down, spread, and thrive.

With the extraordinary expansion of this social activity in the last decade, Cajun dancing can also be found in many places throughout the United States, and even in other countries. Whether it takes place in a house, dance hall, restaurant, or tavern, at a festival or fair, or in a yard or street, we still call a Cajun dance a *fais do-do*.

The Dances of the Cajuns

Cajun dancing belongs to a living tradition. It takes place among a people who have a strong sense of heritage, yet who have proven willing to change, adapt, and evolve. Like all other aspects of their life, the dances of the Cajuns are a blend of languages, cultures, and traditions.

Their ancestors in western France, concentrated in the region around Poitou and southwest of the Loire, entertained themselves, courted, and celebrated the stages of life with a variety of dances. Some were old peasant dances, and some were dances of the nobility, which peasants took as their own. Although we know few details, these dances probably included three forms dating from primitive times: circles, chains, and processionals. As a Celtic people, they also knew reels and jigs. In reels, couples pass between two lines of men and women, linking arms as they swing each other and everyone else in turn; jigs are energetic step dances.

Their Acadian ancestors in Nova Scotia, during the seventeenth and eighteenth centuries, brought their cultural heritage with them from Celtic France. It is possible to reconstruct some of the early dancing of the Acadian colonists from studies of Acadian culture in our century. Some dances were tied to specific religious occasions such as Candlemas and weddings. Some were fast and required a lively tune and a musical instrument such as the fiddle (which had become common in western France before they left for Acadia). On Saturday evenings, Acadians gathered for *les chansons rustiques et la danse*; in 1742 the bishop of Québec wrote a letter complaining about communal gatherings at which men and women danced together.[21] There is little record of Acadian traditions in the early centuries, however, and specific information about their dance steps, tunes, and instruments has not survived.[22]

Hints of early dances in Nova Scotia live on in the style and content of Acadian songs and dances today. The Acadian folk singer Edith Butler observes the close connection between the old and the new: "From the very beginnings until our own days, [our music] is one long succession of *complaintes*, jigs, reels, and songs."[23] Although she is speaking about jigs and reels as types of music, these terms originally meant also the dances they accompanied. The Acadian fiddle tunes played in maritime Canada today are directly descended from their dance music of two and a half centuries ago. Modern Acadians in

Canada perform quadrilles and other square dances and *la gigue* (the jig).

In 1755 large numbers of the Acadians were arrested by the British and expelled from Nova Scotia, an action known as the Grand Dé-rangement. By then the Acadians had probably expanded their store of dances. In addition to the old reels and lively step dances such as jigs and hornpipes, they may have had contredanses, imported from France at some time during the previous century.

During the next ten to thirty years, the exiles were stranded in the British colonies of the Atlantic seaboard and in France and elsewhere. As outcasts who were rejected, feared, and scorned, they had almost no social contact with their hosts. Their fiddles and other delicate instruments did not survive their travels. Nevertheless, as an optimistic and resourceful people, they seized every chance to celebrate. Singing and clapping, they danced at weddings and perhaps also on Saturday nights.[24] Those who arrived in Louisiana in 1765 and later thus brought with them an enduring tradition of dancing.

In colonial Louisiana, the Acadians encountered African slaves and French colonists, their Creole descendants, and American Indians of several nations. After the Louisiana Purchase of 1803, others poured into the territory: mainly Anglo-Americans, but also Scottish, Irish, Germans, Spaniards, Italians, and various African and Caribbean peoples.

Surrounded by this mixture of races and cultures, the Acadian settlers preserved their old dances, but they also tried out many new steps and adopted some of them. From their early neighbors they learned more jigs, hoedowns, and reels. Eventually, in the nineteenth century, they learned the waltz and two-step, quadrilles, and other new dances such as the polka, mazurka, and varsovienne. Many of these dances were brought to the United States by French and Italian dance teachers.

Scholars call this process creolization—absorbing foreign cultures into one's own so that a new culture evolves, based on the past but native-born. Creolization continues to this day. While some dance steps are a century or more old, others have appeared within the last generation. The heritage of the past includes a graceful and flowing style, skill of execution, and courteous respect for the other dancers.

Dances of Yesterday

Three dances of former days, *les danses rondes*, contredanses, and quadrilles, are seldom performed in Acadiana anymore. As entertainments involving large numbers of people in a coordinated and playful

exercise, these dances symbolize the strong and enduring social force
of Cajun life.

Les danses rondes

Circle dances are the oldest dances of the Cajuns, dating from medi-
eval times. They are the *grandpères* and *grandmères* of the family that in
later generations brought forth contredanses, quadrilles, and eventually (after a marriage or two outside the neighborhood) the Cajun
jitterbug. In Acadiana they survived as *les danses rondes,* performed in
house yards on Sundays in Lent. Most of the nineteen play-party
dances collected by Marie del Norte Thériot and Catherine Brookshire
Blanchet in the late 1940s and early 1950s, each attached to a specific
song, are descended from versions in France three hundred or more
years earlier.[25] The Acadian exiles brought them to Louisiana, and the
Cajuns continued to dance them for almost two hundred years. A
distant cousin, the big circle square dance, is still very much alive in the
southern Appalachians.

Les danses rondes are designed for children and easy to perform. Most
are in the form of a single closed circle, usually with partners holding
hands, girl to right of boy. (Two dances in the Thériot-Blanchet collection use parallel lines of boys and girls, as in reels and British contras.)
Sometimes a dancer is in the center of the circle. While the *chanteur* or
chanteuse leads the song, the dancers join in the singing and move
through their paces.

All the figures are traditional. In one simple dance, "La Violette," all
circle right for eight measures, followed by a grand right and left (boys
going right and girls left, taking each other's right and left hands) for
eight measures. In other dances, the boys and girls salute each other,
promenade, swing their partners, choose new partners, clap to the
rhythm, put their left and right feet forward, sit in chairs in the middle, and pass under an arch formed by one couple's hands.

A few of the dances are playful. In "La Petite Boiteuse," a girl in the
center limps with a cane, uses her fingers to suggest the horns of the
devil, and then chases the other dancers until she catches one, who
takes her place in the center. Other songs turn play into courtship. A
boy or girl goes to the center, turns around three times or performs
some other cryptic exercise, and chooses another dancer as a partner.

Dancers today do not need to limit *les danses rondes* to old-time children's songs. They may dance to any rhythmic Cajun music with an
easy beat, almost any waltz or two-step. Following the traditional Cajun
manner, they may perform the steps from memory. In an alternative
manner, similar to that used in quadrilles, someone (perhaps one of
the dancers) may call out instructions: circle right, grand right and left,

swing your partner, and so forth. (For a list of several calls to use in circle dances, see Appendix C.)

Contredanses

In recent years contredanses have enjoyed a modest revival among Cajuns. From time to time groups perform them at festivals, fairs, and other special occasions. These events have included an annual production at the Louisiana Cotton Festival in Ville Platte.

Contredanses have a long and complicated history. They appear to have begun in England, Ireland, and Scotland in the Middle Ages as "country dances" performed by peasants. By the seventeenth century they were the rage in England among the peasantry and bourgeoisie, and they also became popular in British settlements in America. The meaning of the name shifted from "country" (rural) to "counter" (opposite), since the dancers face each other in long lines. Dances known as "contras" have spread from their base in the original British colonies and are taught and performed in many places in North America and wherever square dancing is enjoyed.[26]

Toward the end of the seventeenth century, *contra dances* traveled to France as *contredanses,* which eventually appeared in Nova Scotia and Louisiana. In his novel *Bonaventure,* George Washington Cable refers to Cajun contredanses on Saturday nights and at weddings. When a girl was old enough to move into society—that is, for marriage—she joined the sets of the "contra-dance."[27]

Both British-American contra dances and French contredanses are closely related to quadrilles. Traditionally they involve several couples (eight is common) in a sequence of dance figures, linked either by brief intermissions or by rapid transitions. These figures, and the way they are put together, have varied from time to time and place to place. Some of the numerous versions reflect their origins of hundreds of years ago, and others are recent inventions.

The shape of the dances also varies. Although the oldest and most common form in England is the longway or double-line, many of the French dances are in a circle. Some Cajun contredanses are completely circular, and some combine both shapes. In the longway form, a line of men and a line of women (or two lines of couples) face each other at the start and then dance across and up and down the parallel lines. In the circle form, couples dance around the circle (often reversing direction), across it, and in the center (moving in and out again), and sometimes form a double circle.

Few if any Cajuns still alive have seen an authentic contredanse as it was performed in the early part of this century, and old descriptions are infrequent and vague. Dennis McGee provided as complete an account as exists:

In a contredanse they would form eight couples and they would call, "Family all around!" They would make a round on the floor and when they'd get back to the starting point, they'd reverse direction and come back to the starting point again. The couple dancing together would hold each other, with the girl holding the man's arm, and they would go all around the house. They would do the "back-up" at the same place. The couple faced each other across the room and would do two advancing steps toward each other while dancing. The girl would go get a man and take him to the other side, then she would turn to her partner and station herself with him while the others repeated the same maneuvers. They would advance and meet different partners. They knew what to do. They danced like that at Châtaignier, L'Anse Bourbeuse, and Choupique. These were all places where I lived.[28]

In earlier times the dancers apparently used a springy or sliding walk as they went through the routines. The music is usually an instrumental two-step.

Quadrilles

Quadrilles originated in the French court ballet in the eighteenth century and spread to England. The early French version was for two, four, or more couples, each dancing only with each other. The English version for four couples in a square became the international standard and is one of the ancestors of American square dance. Cajuns probably began to dance English quadrilles in the first half of the nineteenth century, shortly after they became fashionable in New Orleans.

Originally a quadrille consisted of four contredanse figures, with a fifth figure added later. The five figures were usually danced to tunes with different meters, separated by brief intermissions during which the dancers rested and flirted. Any music could be used, so long as it had the right meter and was the right length. By the middle of the nineteenth century, the most popular quadrille was *Les Lanciers* (the Lancers).[29] In the Lancers, the five figures and their meters are "Les Tiroirs" (6/8 or fast waltz), "Les Lignes" (2/4 or polka), "Les Moulinets" (6/8 or fast waltz), "Les Visites" (6/8 or fast waltz), and "Les Lanciers" (4/4 or march time). The last figure ends with a grand march by a column of couples. *Les Lanciers* and other quadrilles were danced by white and black Creoles and Anglo-Americans in New Orleans and by Cajuns in the bayou and prairie countries. Somehow these elegant dances spread and flourished among the backwaters west of the big city.[30]

As late as 1936, Cajun dancers from New Iberia performed a version of *Les Lanciers* at a folk festival in Dallas.[31] By then the dance had become archaic, no longer seen at the community dances on Saturday night but on special occasions pulled out of storage and displayed as a treasured antique.

Like *les danses rondes* and contredanses, quadrilles deserve to be restored among the Cajuns. They continue as popular dances in maritime Canada, with several Acadian villages performing regional variations.[32] Square dancing appeals to many peoples in North America. Cajuns have an opportunity not only to share in a form of entertainment that has proven durable and fun, but to preserve their own distinctive form of it.

Dances of Today

Today the most popular Cajun dances for couples are the waltz, the two-step, and the Cajun jitterbug.[33] When the band plays in triple time (3/4 meter, three beats to a measure, with a strong accent on the first beat), couples dance the waltz. When the band plays in double time (2/4 or 4/4 meter, two or four beats to a measure), they dance either the two-step or the Cajun jitterbug.

By custom, a Cajun band alternates between waltzes and double-time tunes. In some rural dance halls there are more waltzes, to suit the older crowd; in some dance halls in cities and elsewhere, and in progressive zydeco halls, the band plays more two-step music, for those who prefer a faster pace. The troika (for three persons) and the two-couple routine are also performed to two-step music.

Waltz

The waltz became popular in Europe late in the eighteenth century, replacing the aristocratic and highly stylized minuet. After originating in the whirling dances of peasants in Austria and south Germany, the waltz flourished in the ballrooms of the Austrian court, and about 1790 it came into France and England from Alsace. For the next thirty years, a period of great social and political revolution in Europe, the waltz was the rage of England and the Continent, reflecting the new romantic ideal of freedom of expression in emotion and body.[34]

The dance soon came to America and spread swiftly throughout the young nation, including south Louisiana, where the Cajuns on their bayous and streams were not as isolated from cultural trends as many imagine. Most Cajun dancers use the standard method of one long gliding step followed by two steps. The traditional Cajun waltz has none of the spinning motion characteristic of the ballroom version. Although this restrained style persists, it is also common to see couples turn as they dance. In recent years, turnouts, in which the woman turns around under the man's raised arm, have been added to the basic waltz.

In both the waltz and the two-step, the man moves forward and the woman backward, as all the dancers circle the floor counterclockwise. This old-fashioned method of dancing in one direction around the circumference reflects the origins of the waltz and two-step in the ancient circle dances of Europe. It also allows all the dancers to move smoothly in a promenade that flows around the floor.

Two-Step

The two-step appears to have descended from European dances of the early nineteenth century. The most likely ancestor in 2/4 time is the polka, which became an international craze after its introduction in Paris in 1843. The polka has three steps (slide, close, slide) and a hop. Other possible predecessors are African and Caribbean dances brought to Louisiana by blacks in the early years; in Cuba by the 1870s such dances resulted in the rumba, which has the same rhythm as the zydeco two-step, one slow step and two quick ones.

The Cajun two-step has two quick steps (slide, close) and a slow one (slide followed by a touch or pause). Over four beats, the man glides forward with his left foot, brings his right foot together, glides forward with his left foot, and either touches it with his right foot or pauses; then he changes to his right foot. Gliding backward, the woman follows with her opposite foot. Without any turnouts or other flourishes, the two-step retains the simplicity it has had for more than a century.

Until recent years, Cajuns also danced the simpler one-step, especially to slow tunes. It looks like the two-step with one step left out. The man begins with his left foot and brings his right foot together on the second beat; then he changes to his right foot and repeats the move.

Cajun Jitterbug

Just as they absorbed the waltz and the two-step in the nineteenth century, in our own century Cajuns have taken up swing dancing, altered it, and made it their own invention. The resulting dance is called by various names—jig and Breaux Bridge shuffle, to name two—but for consistency we will use the most common term, Cajun jitterbug.

The history of Cajun jitterbug spans about fifty years. In its seminal stage, during the Second World War, young Cajuns simply took over the six-count swing or jitterbug (also called double lindy, after the aviator Charles A. Lindbergh) danced in other parts of the country. A regional refinement of the dance, with an unusual limping step, surfaced in the Lafayette and Opelousas areas about 1970 and soon spread to other parts of south Louisiana, and eventually beyond. During its travels, the dance accumulated a large supply of turns, twists, bends, ducks, and other eye-catching moves.

Cajun jitterbug consists of two skillfully blended parts: a shuffle step and swing moves.

The shuffle step, sometimes called the limp, resembles a limping gait. Every two beats the dancer rises slightly or moves back and forth without the feet leaving the floor. One leg stiffens on the first beat and relaxes on the second beat.

There have been various attempts to explain the origins of the shuffle. According to one account, a man with his leg in a cast came to a dance in Cajun country, and everyone started to copy his limp. The step is similar to the shuffling dances of American Indians, with whom early Cajuns had many social contacts, and it also suggests disco dancing, which started in the 1970s. Dance instructors in the cities have been credited or blamed with inventing the shuffle, but they are responsible mainly for spreading the swing moves that accompany the step.

Part of the puzzle involves the mild syncopation present in Cajun music and dancing. When persons of European descent clap to music and when they dance, most of them prefer to stress the first beat. In Nova Scotia, and especially during the exile and the early years in Louisiana, when musical instruments were seldom available, the Acadians clapped and stamped to keep the rhythm. From the African slaves, Creoles, and American Indians in Louisiana, they learned new dances with the rhythm accented by shuffling and stamping. Somewhere in their musical education, probably from those of African descent, they learned to clap on the second beat. This offbeat rhythm is incorporated into their dance steps, especially the two-step.

The answer may be deceptively simple: the shuffle is the first two steps of the two-step, repeated over and over until the music ends. In the two-step, men start with the left leg, women with the right leg. In the shuffle, most Cajun dancers stiffen or move these same legs on the first of every two beats. (Not all Cajun dancers agree. Some move these legs on the second beat.) The close connection between the two-step and the shuffle allows dancers to shift easily from one dance to the other.

As they shuffle continuously, the dancers hold hands, step apart and come together, and perform elaborate swings involving fast and intricate arm movements.

The origins of these swings are complex and far-flung. Similar moves can be found in some of the old dances of Europe; the *ländler* and other families of dances in the Austrian Tyrol include figures such as the little window (one dance is even called *Das Fenster*) and arms passing behind the back. They can be found in classic American jitter-bug, which first flourished in the 1930s and 1940s, and in the cowboy dances of Texas and the Southwest. The basic open position in Ameri-can jitterbug reappears as the Cajun push and pull, and other adopted moves include the wrap (sweetheart), overhead swing (over the shoul-der), dishrag (windmill), underarm turns, spins, and hand changes behind the back.

Swing moves are eclectic and international, part of the swiftly travel-ing dance lore of peoples everywhere. But swings also appear in the Cajun family tree.

In all the old Cajun dances for groups, couples dance together in a series of prescribed moves. In the Cajun jitterbug, when partners join hands and shuffle side by side, their move is similar to *la promenade* in quadrilles. When they cross hands, they adopt a promenade gesture common in circle and square dances. When they pass around each other, they recall the *dos à dos* (back to back) or *chassez croisé* (sashay across) of quadrilles and other square dances. When they swing or turn together, they make *un tour de mains* (a turn of hands), as in quadrilles. When they cross hands and turn in opposite directions in the windmill, they enact a variant of the dishrag move in *les danses rondes*. And when the music stops, many couples honor each other with the courtly salute (bow and curtsey) with which reels, contredanses, and quadrilles begin.

In recent decades, Cajuns have discovered these and other old swing moves in several attics (not always their own), dusted them off, and given them a fresh and vigorous appearance. In a typical step, the man shuffles in place and leads arm movements while the woman twirls with skirt flaring. Occasionally the man also spins or turns about. The steady shuffle of the dancers beats a counterpoint to their whirls and gestures, as they enact the tension between man and woman, earth and air, old and new, permanence and change.

In some parts of Acadiana, the Cajun jitterbug is called the jig. In most of the western world, the term jig refers to a lively step dance of Celtic origin. The Celtic jig consists of rapid movements of the legs and feet, originally by a single dancer and later by groups. It is no longer seen in Acadiana, although dance teams sometimes perform a closely related step, the Appalachian clog. In Cajun terminology, the jig means a swing dance performed by a couple.

As this last name suggests, the dance sometimes attracts disdain. Some Cajuns reject it as "alien to traditional Cajun dancing,"[35] im-posed upon the local culture by outsiders trying to play Cajun and by citified Cajuns attempting to discover their heritage. Others regard it as an authentic Cajun dance. Perhaps similar dispute occurred in the early nineteenth century when young Cajuns in the bayous and prairies eagerly adopted a romantic new dance from the big city called *la valse*.

Although discouraged in some dance halls, resisted in some towns, and banned among some groups, the Cajun jitterbug has become firmly established in Acadiana. It flourished first in the big cities and among the young; now there are signs that it is spreading in the countryside and among older people. Its exuberance and liveliness commend it to many Cajun dancers, young and old, as well as to outsiders. Hence the conservative reaction.

This book describes the basic shuffle step and twenty-five swing moves, ranging from simple to intricate.

Other Versions and Styles

In Acadiana some dancers perform other versions of the waltz, two-step, and Cajun jitterbug. One waltz is derived from the varsovienne; the man turns the woman so that they dance side by side, holding hands, his right hand on her right shoulder, his left hand in front of his chest. Because of their many contacts with Texas, starting in the 1930s, some Cajuns have fallen under the influence of cowboy dances, now called country western. In the Texas two-step, the man executes a two-step with his left foot and then a one-step with his right foot. Texas swing and the dances of the Creoles continue to influence the Cajun jitterbug. (The influence also works in the other direction, with Texans and blacks adopting aspects of Cajun dancing.)

Every dance floor presents a variety of styles. Some dancers introduce Cajun jitterbug moves into the waltz and waltz moves into the two-step. A man in Mamou is famous for dancing the Texas two-step when the band plays a waltz—and it fits, six steps every two measures. Every region, every village, has its own way of doing the waltz and two-step.

In less attractive variations, some dance against the flow around the dance floor, causing a traffic jam. Others dance to a beat entirely of their own imagination. Individual styles in the Cajun jitterbug range widely, to the point of contortion, and especially in the cities some dancers have adopted eccentricity as the norm. At their most distinctively Cajun, however, the waltz and the two-step follow the standard of inherited tradition, and the Cajun jitterbug has the graceful agility of ballet.

Zydeco Dancing

The zydeco dances of the Creoles are first cousins to Cajun dancing, closely related but distinctively their own. Most Creoles do not circulate around the floor; they dance in place. In the zydeco two-step, they dance slow, quick, quick from side to side, sometimes with a final flick

J. C. Gallow of Mamou teaches the zydeco two-step at the Louisiana Swamp Festival in New Orleans, 1992. (Photo by Ormonde Plater)

of the trailing foot, sometimes turning left or right. In another version, the dancers do the Cajun two-step from side to side.

While waltzing in place, a couple sometimes inserts an old dance called *bes bas* or *basse bas* in the Louisiana Creole language (similar to the Cajun *baisse en bas,* bend down or dip low). On the first beat the dancers take one step to the side, followed by the trailing foot (one, two, pause); they repeat this three times left and three times right (or maybe four times each way), with a pivot turn in between, then go back to the waltz. Creoles call the freeze the zydeco shuffle, and they dance it the same way. Like Cajun dancing, zydeco dancing is not static or changeless. Young Creoles of every generation subtly alter the old dances and sometimes invent steps of their own.

Troika

Cajun dances for three and four persons are popular with groups who go dancing together, and at fairs and festivals. In recent years these dances acquired the name troika, a Russian term similar to the Cajun *trois* or three. Originally in Russia *troika* meant a sleigh drawn by three horses abreast; later it also became the title of a folk dance performed by a man between two women.

In the Cajun troika, a man and two women hold hands and dance a series of figures. Many of these moves are common in international folk dances. One figure, the weave, is taken directly from the Russian troika. Another, the pinwheel, resembles an Austrian and southern German dance called *Spinradl zu Dritt* (spinning wheel for three).

Many times at festivals there are more women than men. The troika is a good way to get more women to join the dancing. It is also fun when two persons know how to dance and one is a novice. If there are tourists, pull them out on the floor and tell them to join hands.

Two-Couple Routine

The two-couple routine involves two men and two women in a series of figures descended from quadrilles, Cajun jitterbug, and international folk dances. A typical quadrille or square dance figure involves only two couples dancing at any one time. Take away the two inactive couples, and the remaining couples are doing a two-couple routine. Both the troika and the two-couple routine are danced to a two-step tune and use the shuffle step of Cajun jitterbug.

This book is about dances presently popular among Cajuns. It describes in detail the waltz, two-step, and Cajun jitterbug, and two group dances, the troika and two-couple routine, as skillful dancers perform them in Acadiana today. These dances are *current* members of the Cajun family. The next generation of Cajuns will change their steps, discover old steps from the past, and create new steps. As always, they will dance whenever the occasion presents itself.

In his talks on Cajun music, folklorist Barry Jean Ancelet likes to quote Dewey Balfa's statement at the 1985 Smithsonian Festival of American Folklife: "Cajun music is like a tree. Its roots have to be watered or it will die. But watering the roots is not all. If a tree is alive, it will grow, and that growth is important, too."[36]

So too with Cajun dancing. Water the roots and let the branches grow.

Notes

1. Told by Leona (Tuti) Guiraid of Catahoula, La., to Patricia K. Rickels.

2. Patricia K. Rickels, "The Folklore of the Acadians," in *The Cajuns: Essays on Their History and Culture*, ed. Glenn R. Conrad (Lafayette, La.: University of Southwestern Louisiana, Center for Louisiana Studies, 1978), 244–46; Jules O. Daigle, *A Dictionary of the Cajun Language* (Ann Arbor, Mich.: Edwards Broth-

ers, Inc., 1984), ix and various word entries.

3. For the background of Cajun music and dancing, see William Faulkner Rushton, *The Cajuns: From Acadia to Louisiana* (New York: The Noonday Press, Farrar, Straus and Giroux, 1979), 231–35; John Broven, *South to Louisiana: The Music of the Cajun Bayous* (Gretna, La.: Pelican Publishing Co., 1983), 11–13; Carl A. Brasseaux, *The Founding of*

New Acadia: The Beginnings of Acadian Life in Louisiana, 1765–1803 (Baton Rouge and London: Louisiana State University Press, 1987), 147–48; Jerry C. Duke, *Dances of the Cajuns* (San Francisco: Duke Publishing Co., [1988]), 13–25; Barry Jean Ancelet, *Cajun Music: Its Origins and Development*, Louisiana Life Series no. 2 (Lafayette, La.: The Center for Louisiana Studies, 1989), 22, 40–41; *J'ai été au bal*, 84 min. videotape (El Cerrito, Calif.: Brazos Films, 1990); Barry Jean Ancelet, Jay Edwards, and Glen Pitre, *Cajun Country* (Jackson, Miss., and London: University Press of Mississippi, 1991), 46–49; Barry Jean Ancelet, "Introduction" in *Cajun Music and Zydeco*, Philip Gould (Baton Rouge and London: Louisiana State University Press, 1991), ix–xxi.

4. C. C. Robin, *Voyage to Louisiana*, trans. Stuart O. Landry, Jr. (New Orleans: Pelican Publishing Co., 1966), 115. Tafia is a rum made from distilled sugarcane juice.

5. For a description of an old-time *fais do-do*, see Lauren C. Post, *Cajun Sketches from the Prairies of Southwest Louisiana* (Baton Rouge: Louisiana State University Press, 1974), 152–57.

6. Rickels, "The Folklore of the Acadians," 247; Raymond E. François, *Yé Yaille, Chère: Traditional Cajun Dance Music* (Lafayette, La.: Thunderstone Press, 1990), 94.

7. Post, *Cajun Sketches*, 156.

8. Ann Allen Savoy, *Cajun Music: A Reflection of a People*, 3rd ed. (Eunice, La.: Bluebird Press, 1988), 240.

9. Carolyn Ramsey, *Cajuns on the Bayou* (New York: Hastings House, 1957), 121–23; Ormonde Plater, "The Hurricane of Chênière Caminada: A Narrative Poem in French," *Louisiana Folklore Miscellany* 3, no. 2 (April 1971): 6–7.

10. Barry Jean Ancelet and Elemore Morgan, Jr., *The Makers of Cajun Music: Musiciens cadiens et créoles* (Austin: University of Texas Press, 1984), 35.

11. François, *Yé Yaille, Chère*, 3.

12. Broven, *South to Louisiana*, 13.

13. Daigle, *A Dictionary of the Cajun Language*, xii; Gwendolyn Midlo Hall, *Africans in Colonial Louisiana: The Development of Afro-Creole Culture in the Eighteenth Century* (Baton Rouge and London: Louisiana State University Press, 1992), 157–58.

14. Hall, *Africans in Colonial Louisiana*, 294, 320, 379–80.

15. As defined by Rockin' Dopsie (Alton Rubin), in Savoy, *Cajun Music*, 363.

16. For details, see Macon Fry and Julie Posner, *Cajun Country Guide* (Gretna, La.: Pelican Publishing Co., 1992).

17. Savoy, *Cajun Music*, 275.

18. François, *Yé Yaille, Chère*, 3–4. Used by permission.

19. Ibid., 226, 239.

20. Ibid., 223.

21. Rushton, *The Cajuns*, 231.

22. See Anselme Chiasson, "Traditions and Oral Literature in Acadia," in *The Acadians of the Maritimes: Thematic Studies*, ed. Jean Daigle (Moncton, N.B.: Centre d'études acadiennes, Université de Moncton, 1982), 504–5. For dancing in a small fishing community founded soon

after the exile, see Anselme Chiasson, *Chéticamp: Histoire et Traditions acadiennes,* 4th ed. (Richibouctou, N.B.: Les Editions Babineau, 1990), 210, 212, 236.

23. Edith Butler, *L'Acadie sans frontières* (Ottawa: Les Editions Leméac, 1977), 15: "Depuis les touts débuts jusqu'à nos jours, c'est une longue suite de complaintes, de gigues, de reels et de chansons." A *complainte* is a long song telling a story about a people's heritage.

24. For an account of a wedding dance among the exiles, see Gabriel Debien, "The Acadians in Santo Domingo," in *The Cajuns,* ed. Conrad, 46.

25. Marie del Norte Thériot and Catherine Brookshire Blanchet, *Les Danses Rondes: Louisiana French Folk Dances* (Abbeville, La.: R. E. Blanchet, Distributor, 1955); repr. Brain Dance Ink, P.O. Box 681264, San Antonio, TX 78250.

26. Jane A. Harris, Anne M. Pittman, and Marlys S. Waller, *Dance a While: Handbook of Folk, Square, Contra, and Social Dance,* 6th ed. (New York: Macmillan Publishing Co., 1988), 165–69.

27. George W. Cable, *Bonaventure: A Prose Pastoral of Acadian Louisiana* (New York: Charles Scribner's Sons, 1888), 10, 13.

28. François, *Yé Yaille, Chère,* 8–9.

29. Harris, Pittman, and Waller, *Dance a While,* 4.

30. See J. Vegas, *Les Lanciers: le véritable quadrille anglais* (New Orleans: L. Gabici, 1857), William Ransom Hogan Jazz Archive of the Howard-Tilton Library at Tulane University. This sheet music has dance calls in French and English.

31. Post, *Cajun Sketches,* 155. He names the five parts as "L'Avance," "Petit Salut," "Grand Salut," "Les Visites," and "Grandes Chaînes." Post mentions another square dance, in four parts, called *Les Variétés,* 156.

32. *Les Lanciers* is still danced in Neguac, New Brunswick. Another village dance, *Quadrille de Barachois,* has been recorded in Barachois, N.B., by the Moncton council of the Centre de Recherches et d'Information Folkloriques de Montréal. We are indebted to René Babineau of Richibouctou, N.B., for copies of the instructions to both dances.

33. For a survey of popular Cajun dances, see Duke, *Dances of the Cajuns,* 27–39.

34. Paul Nettl, *The Story of Dance Music* (New York: Philosophical Library, 1947), 252–55, and Eduard Reeser, *The History of the Waltz* (Stockholm: The Continental Book Co. A.B., n.d.), 27–28.

35. A decision reached by the Houston Heritage Chapter of the Cajun French Music Association on 29 Feb. 1992, reported in the CFMA newsletter, *La Voix des Cadjins,* April 1992.

36. Ancelet, *Cajun Music,* 50.

Starting to Dance

On vous invite pour le bal à soir
mais là-bas à Grand Mamou.
On vous invite tout pour le gros bal
mais tout l'temps en l'autour du moyeu.

We invite you to the dance tonight
over there in Big Mamou.
We invite you to the big dance
all the time around the hub.

—From "La chanson de Mardi Gras," the traditional
Mardi Gras song at Mamou.

So let's go to the dance! Try out the steps at home. Practice with different partners. Watch skilled dancers. Go to the dance halls, restaurants, clubs, bars, lounges, parties, fairs, and festivals where people dance to Cajun and zydeco music. Look, listen, and above all, dance.

Start with the most basic Cajun dances, the waltz and the two-step. Many dancers, especially out in the country, use only these old steps and nothing else. When you have learned them, advance to the more difficult Cajun jitterbug.

Here are a few tips to make dancing easy:

1. Relax and Have Fun

The primary reason people want to learn Cajun dancing is to have fun. Regardless of how good or bad you think you are, having fun should be your main goal. Hopefully you're dancing to relieve stress rather than to create stress. Try to be patient and enjoy yourself. The proper attitude will make a world of difference in your ultimate enjoyment of dancing.

Dancing is not a competitive sport, and there is no final exam to worry about once you step on the dance floor. Once you begin dancing in public, you are certain to see dancers with diverse abilities—from recent beginners to seasoned professionals. While the professionals are wonderful to watch and an inspiration to beginners, try not to let someone else's dance ability make you overly competitive or self-conscious. The main focus should be on having fun. People come in a variety of shapes and sizes, and the way you dance with your partner is

45

unique to the two of you. What matters is that you and your partner are having a good time together. The rest will come with time.

As you begin to feel comfortable and confident, you'll naturally want to pay more attention to details and work on learning new steps. As the old adage goes, practice makes perfect. With practice, you'll soon find that you no longer have to concentrate continually on what your feet or hands should be doing. Thus, you can enjoy the music more, and you'll begin to feel the rhythm and beat in your movement.

In addition, you are laying down a foundation for yourself. The more you know, the more enjoyable the dancing becomes. In the Cajun jitterbug, for example, as you add new moves to your repertoire, you can alter the sequence or combination of moves to make the dance itself unique to you and your partner.

2. Listen to the Beat of the Music

As in any style of dancing, it is important that you hear the beat of the music. Before you even step onto the dance floor, take a moment to listen for the beat of the song. Listening for the drums, guitar, or triangle will help you pick out the beat.

Cajun music is divided into two basic groups—waltzes and two-steps. The odds are fifty-fifty that a song will be either a waltz or a two-step. The basic difference between the two is that waltzes are generally much slower than two-steps. Even though most two-steps are faster, a few Cajun songs such as "The Pine Grove Blues" are slow, easy two-steps.

Waltzes have three even beats and are done to 3/4 or waltz time rhythm. The count for a waltz is a slow, steady 1-2-3, 1-2-3. Also, the heavy or accented beat is on the "1" count. Two-steps have four beats and are performed to 4/4 or common time rhythm. The count for the two-step is a fast, steady 1-2-3-4, 1-2-3-4. In the two-step, the accented beats are on the "2" and "4" counts. Keeping an ear to the percussion instruments will help you pick out the beat and count the music time easily.

It is essential that you and your partner be on the same beat when you dance. Otherwise, the two of you are destined to stumble around the room feeling totally miserable. If either you or your partner feels off the beat, the best thing to do is stop, listen to the beat of the music, then start again. If you still have difficulty hearing the beat, try playing tapes or CDs of Cajun music at home. Turn up the bass to the song and tap your foot or clap your hands to the music. Soon the beat will become part of you, and you won't have to think about it.

3. Learn How to Lead and How to Follow

Traditionally, in Cajun as in most other dancing, the man leads and the woman follows. This alleviates any confusion on the dance floor. Since the role of each person is clearly defined, the two must work together as a team. Communication between the two is important. The leader must be able to tell his partner what to do by using his hands and body. Likewise, the follower has to understand what he is telling her. Just how well each partner accomplishes this task will determine how smooth the two of them look together.

A good leader is one who doesn't yank or jerk his partner in the direction he wants her to go. A good follower is one who responds well to her partner's lead.

As the leader, the man should always step first with his left foot. He should also start off slow and easy with a new partner. The leader is also responsible for starting on the correct beat and maintaining the rhythm throughout the dance. As the leader, he also decides what moves the couple will do and should stick to those moves he is comfortable doing. He should make sure that they don't bump into people or things as they dance.

The woman always steps first with her right foot. As the follower, she should not attempt to lead. Frequently, she may find that she is given a weak or poor lead. In such a case, she tries to compensate, if possible, by keeping slight tension in her arms. By watching her partner for signals and gestures, she is able to anticipate his lead and let him guide her through the moves.

Both the leader and the follower should know what his or her role is before starting to dance. If you still feel awkward after you've begun, don't be afraid to ask your partner to help you find out what you're doing right or wrong. At no time, however, should either partner criticize the other! We're supposed to be having fun, right?

4. Learn How to Communicate with Your Partner

Communication is nothing more than sharing information with one another. As you learn each dance move, you'll discover that the man uses certain signals to let his partner know what he is about to do. Likewise, the woman watches for his signals and gestures and automatically responds by taking appropriate steps. It is important, therefore, that the man give clear signals to the woman and do so early enough for her to react in time.

Whether you're dancing a traditional waltz, two-step, or Cajun jitter-bug, it's important to remember that you and your partner are working as a team. Unlike the disco dancing of the 1970s that was done inde-pendently of a partner, Cajun dancing requires that you and your partner move together. You'll find that you'll get the most out of the music and dancing when both of you are *connected* or really moving together. Dancing smoothly and fluidly comes about when the part-ners are able to communicate with one another. This will ultimately make you a better dancer and set you apart from the rest of the crowd.

One of the most obvious ways we communicate is by speaking. It's perfectly natural that you may want to talk with your partner while you dance, whether it's about the moves, the music, or whatever. On occa-sion, a band may be so loud that you find it difficult to talk with your partner over the music. Thus, nonverbal communication with the hands and eyes becomes necessary.

The use of your hands allows you to *talk* to your partner as you dance. Using your hands lets you communicate the moves, rhythm, energy, and direction to your partner. This is especially important for the man, since he is responsible for giving his partner a decent lead. The woman, too, will benefit as a follower when she *listens* for his lead through the hands.

Finally, the eyes are another subtle way to communicate with your partner. Next time you're out where people are dancing, notice how couples look at one another. For some strange reason, many dancers avoid each other's eyes while they dance. The sad thing is that they wind up missing out on much of the fun of dancing. They appear totally disinterested in their partners. Looking at your partner helps do several things. First, it's fun! You'll relax and enjoy the dancing more if you begin to look at your partner. Next, you'll pick up on cues more readily, particularly in fast moves such as in Cajun jitterbug. Finally, the overall look of your dancing will be improved. Those watching you dance will notice that you and your partner are moving together and having fun. Remember, smiling can hide a multitude of mistakes when you're dancing. Don't be upset if you miss a beat or mess up a move. It's not the end of the world! Those dancers who can smile and laugh through a poor move will look ten times better than those who have a pained or agonized look on their faces.

As you begin to learn new moves, remember to keep the dancing simple at first. It's not the number of moves that will make you a polished dancer, but the quality of your moves. Couples who are smiling and dancing smoothly together will always outshine others who try to show off everything they know.

5. Watch Your Weight and Balance

Dancing is much like walking. Your weight is transferred from one foot to another in an alternating fashion. In walking, we all take this for granted, but in dancing some people let this become a difficult learning experience. It's really very simple.

As you learn a new move, try to be conscious of just where your weight should be and how it changes from step to step. When dancing, always remember that you put your weight on the leading foot. For example, in the waltz, the man first steps forward with his left foot and the woman steps back with her right foot. The weight should then be transferred from one foot to the other as you proceed through the movement. Also, your weight should be slightly forward, on the balls of your feet, not on your heels. When done correctly, you'll feel a sense of balance in your dance steps.

Notice as you watch experienced dancers doing a waltz or two-step that they are gliding smoothly on the balls of their feet. The dancers do not pick up their feet but slide them in a gliding motion across the floor. Bending the knees slightly will help you to keep your weight slightly forward with the heels barely off the floor.

The effect you are trying to create while dancing is one that is smooth and effortless. Your steps, therefore, should be smooth and light.

6. Exercise Common Sense and Courtesy When Dancing

Now that Cajun music and dancing have become popular, people are sometimes packed like sardines in clubs and dance halls. With this crowding, it's important to respect other dancers on the floor by not intruding on their space, stepping on their feet, or bulldozing into people. Wild dancing or dancing against the flow of the other dancers is rude behavior.

Traditionally, the waltz and two-step are done in a circular motion counterclockwise around the room. This custom helps avoid confusion and creates a nice, orderly flow of people around the room. Those couples who overtake others should pass on the inside or outside so as not to bump into people. As the leader, the man is responsible for steering his partner safely around the floor and not bumping her into others. Should he see that he is about to bump into someone or something, he should pull back on his partner to avoid the collision and then go into a conversational step where he rocks back and forth before proceeding.

Often when a band performs a lively two-step, some couples will choose to dance a traditional two-step, and others will opt for the Cajun jitterbug. Couples who prefer to do the two-step should stay along the perimeter or outside of the dance floor as they move in a circle. Those couples who choose to do the Cajun jitterbug should move to the center of the room so as not to impede the normal flow of dancers who are two-stepping. This convention allows for freedom of movement for both styles of dancing.

Should you happen to bump accidentally into someone on a crowded dance floor, it is considered rude not to stop and apologize for your behavior. Common sense dictates that you at least check on the person or persons you bump into and do your best to refrain from bumping into others again even if it means moving to an area that is less crowded.

7. Wear the Right Shoes and Clothing

When going out dancing, it is best to dress for the occasion. Cool, lightweight clothing is generally a wise idea for most outdoor festivals, as well as some crowded dance halls. The temperature, humidity, and how much dancing you plan to do are all factors to consider when deciding what to wear. Some of the older clubs in south Louisiana even have an unwritten dress code (no hats, no shorts, etc.), which may be another factor to consider when you go out.

For most indoor dance conditions, it is best to avoid shoes with rubbery or sticky soles such as tennis shoes or deck shoes. Such shoes tend to grip most wood and tile floors and make it difficult for you to slide easily when you dance. Instead, you will find that shoes with a smooth leather sole will be best for most purposes when dancing indoors. Some of the old dance halls frequently sprinkle cornmeal on the floor to make it easier for the dancers to glide across the floor. High heels are not recommended for women, since they tend to make dancing more difficult. Women generally seem to prefer comfortable leather flats for dancing.

When dancing at outdoor festivals, almost anything goes. You'll see T-shirts, jeans, shorts, and tennis shoes worn at most festivals featuring Cajun music and dancing.

I. Traditional Dances for Couples

In the traditional waltz and two-step, the dancers hold each other in the closed dance position. Slightly apart, they face each other, looking over the other's right shoulder. With his left hand, raised about shoulder high, the man holds the woman's right hand. His right hand holds her left waist, and her left hand rests on his right shoulder.

Most Cajuns perform the waltz and two-step like a stately walk. Keeping the upper part of their bodies motionless, they move mostly with their legs, knees slightly bent, gliding on the balls of their feet. Their feet barely leave the floor. With the man moving forward and the woman backward, all the couples dance in a counterclockwise direction around the dance floor. Couples occasionally make turns during which they move backward and forward, and in the waltz the woman sometimes turns out in a circle.

There are several regional and ethnic variations in style. Older people in rural Acadiana often dance cheek to cheek. Some Cajuns move their shoulders and arms in a rocking motion. Many Creoles stomp and use intricate foot moves. Especially near the Texas border, where country-western styles influence Cajun dancing, couples move from side to side and lift their feet off the floor. Where space permits, couples sometimes move at random on the dance floor, turning in circles.

A. Waltz

On the first accented beat (of three), the man glides forward with his left foot, and follows with two steps, right and left (L-2-3). At the same time, the woman glides back with her right foot, and follows with two steps, left and right (R-2-3). On the next accented beat (of three), they start on the other foot.

They move in a counterclockwise direction around the floor, he forward and she backward. At the corners, moving forward and backward, they may turn counterclockwise. When there is room, the woman may make a turnout in which the man raises his left hand and she turns around once or twice to the right (dropping her left hand to get it out of the way), while he continues straight ahead or turns around once to the left.

Social dance position. *Face each other. Men, take her right hand with your left hand and put your right hand on her waist.*

As they begin to waltz, the couple sometimes uses a conversational step. The man goes forward L-2-3 and back R-2-3, while the woman mirrors his steps (back R-2-3 and forward L-2-3). Eventually, they break out into the normal waltz pattern. This step is also useful in a crowd, where the couple may mark time or rock back and forth, while waiting to break out.

Basic Waltz

Man	Woman
• through every six beats:	• through every six beats:
(1) L forward	(1) R back
(2) R forward	(2) L back
(3) L short	(3) R short
(1) R forward	(1) L back
(2) L forward	(2) R back
(3) R short	(3) L short

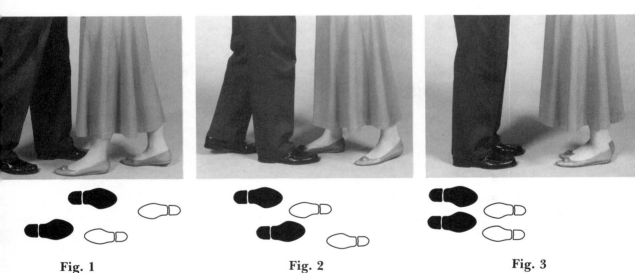

Fig. 1   **Fig. 2**   **Fig. 3**

Fig. 1. Left. *Men, start with your left foot and slide forward. Ladies, start with your right foot and slide backward.*

Fig. 2. . . . two. *Men, slide your right foot forward. Ladies, slide your left foot backward.*

Fig. 3. . . . three. *And bring the other foot together.*

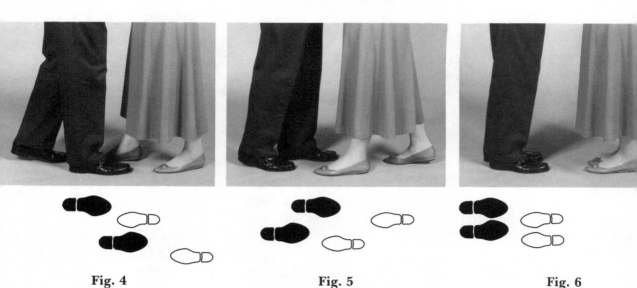

Fig. 4   **Fig. 5**   **Fig. 6**

Fig. 4. Right. *Men, continue with your right foot, sliding forward. Ladies, continue with your left foot, sliding backward.*

Fig. 5. . . . two. *Men, slide your left foot forward. Ladies, slide your right foot backward.*

Fig. 6. . . . three. *And bring the other foot together.*

Waltz Turns and Turnouts

turn
- push and pull her in a slow turn to the left, forward L-2-3 and back R-2-3, while turning counterclockwise

turnout
- as L foot moves forward, raise L hand and pull her left waist with R hand, turning her

double turnout
- raise L hand for 1st turn
- keep L hand up for 2nd turn

turn
- he pushes and pulls you in a slow turn to the left, back R-2-3 and forward L-2-3, while turning counter-clockwise

turnout
- as R foot moves back, he raises your R hand and pulls your left waist
- turn around right R-2-3
- meanwhile, drop L hand

double turnout
- turn around right R-2-3
- turn around right L-2-3

Waltz around the floor. *Relax, this is supposed to be fun! See how different we all are? That's the beauty, and the earlier you find it out, the better.*

Start the turnout. *Men, lift your left hand above her head, open your palm, and she will pivot around your hand. Don't squeeze her hand.*

Keep turning. *Ladies, drop your hand to your side or behind your back. This serves two purposes: your hand gets out of the way, and the move looks pretty. Keep moving back; don't slow down.*

End the turnout. *Men, if you're crowded and can't turn her out, just shuffle in place or rock back and forth. Pressure with your right hand gives her the signal. To make her turn more than once, keep your hand up. Ladies, to stop him from turning you too much, lower his hand.*

In a triple turnout, first the woman turns. *As you step back on your left foot, turn right as in the simple turnout.*

. . . and then the man turns. *As you start forward on your right foot, pivot to the left. Ladies, you can tell he is turning when he makes this move.*

combination turnout
• raise L hand for turn and then turn around left R-2-3

triple turnout
• raise L hand for 1st turn and then turn around left R-2-3
• keep L hand up for 2nd turn

turnout in double-time waltz
• raise L hand for turn

combination turnout
• turn around right R-2-3 and then step back L-2-3

triple turnout
• turn around right R-2-3 and then step back L-2-3
• turn around right R-2-3

turnout in double-time waltz
• turn around right R-2-3-4-5-6 making only one turn

B. Two-Step

   On the first beat (of four), the man glides forward with his left foot, brings his right foot together, glides forward with his left foot, and touches it with his right foot (L-2-L-4). At the same time, the woman glides back with her right foot, brings her left foot together, glides back with her right foot, and touches it with her left foot (R-2-R-4). On the next first beat (of four), they start on the other foot.

They move in a counterclockwise direction around the floor, he forward and she backward. At the corners, moving forward and backward, they may turn counterclockwise. (There are no turnouts in the two-step.)

As they begin to dance the two-step, the couple sometimes uses a conversational step. The man goes forward L-2-L-4 and back R-2-R-4, while the woman mirrors his steps (back R-2-R-4 and forward L-2-L-4). Eventually, they break out into the normal two-step pattern. This step is also useful in a crowd, where the couple may mark time or rock back and forth, while waiting to break out.

Basic Two-Step

Man	**Woman**
• through every eight beats:	• through every eight beats:

Man	Woman
(1) L forward	(1) R back
(2) R together	(2) L together
(3) L forward	(3) R back
(4) R touches L	(4) L touches R
(1) R forward	(1) L back
(2) L together	(2) R together
(3) R forward	(3) L back
(4) L touches R	(4) R touches L

Left. *Men, start with your left foot and slide forward. Ladies, start with your right foot and slide backward.*

. . . **together.** *And slide your other foot together. Every other step is accented (the second and fourth beats).*

. . . left. *Men, slide your left foot forward. Ladies, slide your right foot backward.*

. . . touch. *And slide your other foot for a brief touch.*

Right. *Men, continue with your right foot, sliding forward; ladies, with your left foot sliding backward.*

. . . together. *And slide your other foot together.*

. . . right. *Men, slide your right foot forward. Ladies, slide your left foot backward.*

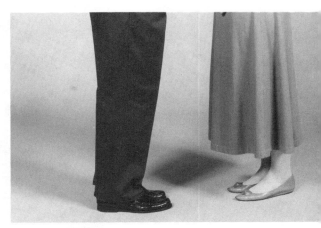

. . . touch. *And slide your other foot for a brief touch.*

Two-step around the floor. *Same closed position as in the waltz. Slide-slide-slide-touch, 1-2-3-touch. It's three steps and a pause while you touch your feet together.*

To turn, go forward. *Men, go forward on the left-2-3-touch. Turns follow the same principles as with the waltz. You turn at the corners of the dance floor.*

. . . and go back. *Men, go back on the right-2-3-touch. The shorter your steps are, the easier it is to make the turn.*

Two-Step Turns

turn
- push and pull her in a slow turn to the left, forward L-2-L-4 and back R-2-R-4, while turning counterclockwise

turn
- he pushes and pulls you in a slow turn to the left, back R-2-R-4 and forward L-2-L-4, while turning counterclockwise

II. Cajun Jitterbug

During a tune lasting three minutes or more, a couple dances several different steps at random. The man decides which step to use and leads the woman through the swing moves making up the step. Many steps include five parts:

(1) *Start*. The dancers use turns and arm movements to get into position. This action is often energetic, and they usually touch each other only with their hands.

(2) *Shuffle*. Once in position, they travel in a straight line or turn in a circle. This action is usually more relaxed, and they touch each other side to side.

(3) *Reverse*. They use turns and arm movements to change position, usually facing in the opposite direction. This action is often energetic, and they usually touch each other only with their hands.

(4) *Shuffle*. Once in the new position, they travel in a straight line or turn in a circle, usually in the opposite direction. They touch each other side to side.

(5) *Release*. Moving apart, they release hands or use turns and arm movements to end the dance step, facing each other. Then they begin a new step, sometimes immediately, sometimes after a break during which they use the push and pull move.

Other steps include only *start, shuffle,* and *release,* or simply *start* and *release*.

As in the traditional dances, style is important. Dancers glide their feet over the surface of the floor. While establishing their own space on the dance floor, they respect the presence of other dancers. They hold hands loosely so that they can turn while maintaining touch. They move gracefully and easily, as a pair of equals. When shuffling side by side or turning together in a circle, they look in each other's eyes. When the music ends, the men bow and the women curtsey.

In the following descriptions, first we briefly portray each dance step. Then we break down the step into detailed parts, in parallel columns for the man and the woman.

A. J. and Faith Blake dance the Cajun jitterbug at the Louisiana Swamp Festival, 1992. (Photo by Ormonde Plater)

A. Shuffle Step

During swing moves, the dancers shuffle with a limping, up-and-down step. They push up slightly (or glide forward or back) on the first beat and drop slightly on the second beat. Normally the man starts on the left foot and the woman on the right. They may start on the other foot, or change to it, so long as they do not lose the beat during the swing move.

Up on the first beat. *Men usually go up (or slide forward) on their left foot, down on their right. Women usually go up (or slide forward) on their right foot, down on their left.*

Shuffle in the jitterbug. *Remember when you were young and had a hobby horse. One foot goes up (or forward) and the other goes down, up and down, slide-down.*

. . . and down on the second. *These are the more comfortable positions for most men and women, but some prefer the other foot. If you can shuffle with either foot, so much the better. That way you can alternate, and your legs won't give out.*

Man	Woman
• through every two beats:	• through every two beats:
(1) L push up (or move)	(1) R push up (or move)
(2) R down	(2) L down

B. Swing Moves

The following twenty-five swing moves are more than enough to take a couple through a tune of about three minutes.

The first eight swing moves (Push and Pull, Side-by-Side, two versions of Sweetheart, Reverse Sweetheart, Around the Waist, Over the Shoulder, and Bend and Turn) begin with the dancers facing each other and holding hands loosely.

Push and Pull

In this move, the dancers rest, mark time, or prepare for the next swing move.

The man's right hand holds the woman's left hand, and his left hand holds her right hand. He pushes and pulls her with alternate hands, through four beats, while their feet follow. Meanwhile they move slowly in a clockwise turn. To start the next swing move, the man falls back at arm's length.

Man	Woman
• face her	• face him
• hold hands, palms up	• hold hands, palms down
• through every four beats:	• through every four beats:
(1) L back (while L hand pulls and R pushes)	(1) R forward (as he pulls R hand and pushes L)
(2) R down	(2) L down
(3) L forward (while L hand pushes and R pulls)	(3) R back (as he pushes R hand and pulls L)
(4) R down	(4) L down
• while both turn slowly right	• while both turn slowly right

Push and pull. *Ladies, if you don't know where he is with his steps, just go up and down in place until you figure it out. Men, if you use your hands to push and pull, she won't have that problem.*

Step back. *Men, step back with the left foot. While you push and pull, slowly you move in a circle to the right. Your right foot is the pivot, making little steps. Ladies, you mirror his movements. When he steps back, you step forward.*

. . . and step forward. *Men, step forward with the left foot. The shorter your steps are, the easier it is to follow the beat. Ladies, your left foot is the pivot, making little steps. You turn slowly to the right.*

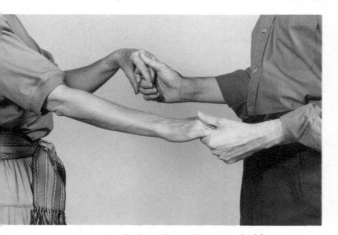 

Left hand pull. *Men, hold your hands waist high, with your palms up. Ladies, place your hands with palms down in his hands.*

. . . and push. *Look at the upper part of your partner's body. Your hands will tell your feet what to do.*

Side-by-Side

Pulling with his right hand, and turning to the left, the man draws the woman to his right side, so that they face in the same direction. They hold their inside hands with forearms upright, touching each other, with the elbows resting on their other hands. They shuffle back and forth. To reverse direction, he pulls with his left hand, pushes out with his right hand, and both turn around to the inside. They shuffle again. To release, he pulls away.

Man

start
- turning to left, pull R hand to your side and raise forearm

- rest R elbow on your L hand

shuffle
- shuffle forward and back

reverse
- turning to right, pull L hand in and raise forearm

- rest L elbow on your R hand

Woman

start
- turning you to right, he pulls your L hand to his side and raises your forearm

- rest L elbow on your R hand

shuffle
- shuffle forward and back

reverse
- turning you to left, he pulls your R hand in and raises your forearm

- rest R elbow on your L hand

Rock back. *The starting position for many jitterbug moves. Hold hands and rock back.*

Shuffle side by side. *Hold her close to you. Keep your forearms upright and touching each other.*

Reverse to the other side. *Turn around and pull your other arm in. Look at each other's eyes as you shuffle.*

Pull away. *To release, pull away and face each other.
Then you're ready for the next move. Ladies, you just shuffle
in place, while he steps back at arm's length. Don't try to
follow him.*

shuffle
• shuffle forward and back

release
• pull away and face her

shuffle
• shuffle forward and back

release
• he pulls away and you face
  him

Sweetheart

The man raises his left hand and rotates it, palm out and thumb
down. The woman turns left under his arm one-half turn and wraps
herself against his right side, both facing in the same direction. They
hold their outside hands together in front of them. After a few shuffles
back and forward, he shifts her to his left side, using the inner side of
his right forearm. They shuffle some more, and he shifts her to his
right side. They turn in a clockwise direction, holding their front
hands out. To release her, he drops his front (left) hand, while she
spins right. They end up facing each other.

Man

start
• raise L hand and rotate it with
  palm out and thumb down
• wrap her under it, cradled
  against your R arm, and lower
  L arm

Woman

start
• when he raises your R hand,
  turn left under it, cradled
  against his R arm, and lower
  your R arm

Raise your left hand. *Men, raise your left hand about shoulder high and rotate your hand, palm out with your thumb down.*

. . . and wrap her on your right side. *Ladies, when he raises your right hand, turn left. Men, once she turns, lower your left hand.*

Shuffle back and forth. *When you shuffle, stay shoulder to shoulder so you can go up and down together. Use short steps.*

Shift her to your left side. *When you reach the farthest point, use the pressure of your right elbow to slide her to the left side. Shuffle a bit, then shift her back to the right.*

shuffle
- shuffle back and forward

reverse
- after you move forward, shift her to left side

shuffle
- shuffle back and forward

release
- after you move forward, shift her to right side and hold L hand out, palm up
- turn clockwise moving forward

shuffle
- shuffle back and forward

reverse
- after you move forward, he shifts you to his left side

shuffle
- shuffle back and forward

release
- after you move forward, he shifts you to his right side and holds your R hand out
- turn clockwise moving back

Spin her out. *In a right turn, the woman goes forward and the man back. To release her, always drop the hand out in front of you. This time it's the left hand. Ladies, after you spin out, shuffle in place until you figure out which foot he is on.*

- drop L hand and she spins right
- L hand take her R hand and face her

- when he drops your R hand, spin right
- he takes your R hand and you face him

Sweetheart (Variation)

In the *reverse* and *release*, instead of shifting the woman to the other side, the man raises both hands and unwinds her in a full turn until she reaches his other side, where he lowers his hands and she cradles against his arm.

Man

start
- same as above

shuffle
- same as above

reverse
- raise both hands over head and turn her in right turn to your left side
- lower both arms and wrap L arm around her

shuffle
- same as above

Woman

start
- same as above

shuffle
- same as above

reverse
- he raises both hands over head and turns you right 1 turn to his left side
- cradle against his L arm

shuffle
- same as above

He raises hands and she turns. *This is a fancy way to move the woman. Ladies, you unwind in a right turn and shift to his left side.*

. . . and settles on his left. *You're in the sweetheart position again, but on the other side of each other.*

Raise hands and she turns again.
Ladies, you unwind in a left turn and settle on his right side.

Turning with hands out. *When you turn in a circle, pick out an earlobe or collar to look at. This prevents you from getting dizzy, and you look as if you're having fun.*

release
- raise both hands over head and turn her in left turn to your right side
- lower both arms and wrap R arm around her
- hold L hand out, palm up
- turn clockwise moving forward
- drop L hand and she spins right
- L hand take her R hand and face her

release
- he raises both hands over head and turns you left 1 turn to his right side
- cradle against his R arm

- he holds your R hand out
- turn clockwise moving back

- when he drops your R hand, spin right
- he takes your R hand and you face him

Reverse Sweetheart

The man frees his right hand. Turning to the left, he raises his hand above the woman's right arm. Cradled in her right arm, he takes her left hand, and they hold their outside hands in front of them. After a few turns to the right, he drops his right hand and spins right until he faces her and takes her left hand again.

Man	**Woman**
start	*start*
• free R hand and turn left, crossing R hand over her arm	• he drops your L hand and turns left into your right side
• R hand take her L hand (she on left, behind you, touching your left shoulder)	• he takes your L hand (you on left, behind him, with your right shoulder touching his left shoulder)
shuffle	*shuffle*
• backing up, turn clockwise	• moving forward, turn clockwise
release	*release*
• drop R hand and spin right	• he drops your L hand and spins right
• R hand take her L hand and face her	• he takes your L hand and you face him

Start turning left. *Men, when you step back, drop your right hand. Then turn to the left, holding your right hand above her arm.*

. . . and wrap yourself against her. *With her behind you and to the left, take her left hand.*

Turn clockwise. *Turn to the right with hands out in front. The man backs up, the woman goes forward.*

Spin out. *When you're ready to release her, drop your right hand out in front and spin out to the right. Then join hands and go back to the basic step.*

Around the Waist

With both hands, the man pulls the woman to his right side, and they hold hands against the outside of each other's waist. After a few turns to the right, he pulls away. He then pulls her to his left side, and they make a few turns to the left. To release, he turns right, pulling her at the waist with his left hand and turning her to the left. They make a full turn away from each other and rejoin hands.

Man

start
- hold both her hands and pull her to your right side
- place R hand on outside of her L waist and L hand palm out on outside of your L waist

shuffle
- moving forward, turn clockwise

Woman

start
- he holds both your hands and pulls you to his right side
- he places your R hand on outside of his L waist and your L hand palm out on outside of your L waist

shuffle
- moving forward, turn clockwise

Hold hands and rock back. *Start with the basic push and pull step. Men, when you're ready, rock back at arm's length.*

Hold the waist. *Your right hand covers your partner's hand on the waist. Your left hand rests palm out on your waist. Then turn clockwise.*

To reverse, step back. *When you reverse, first step back at arm's length. Then pull her to your other side.*

Hold the waist. *Your left hand covers your partner's hand on the waist. Your right hand rests palm out on your waist. Then turn counterclockwise.*

reverse
- release her and pull away
- pull her to your left side
- place L hand on outside of her R waist and R hand palm out on outside of your R waist

shuffle
- moving forward, turn counter-clockwise

release
- drop her L hand and turn right
- L hand pulls her at the waist into left turn
- R hand takes her L hand, and L hand takes her R hand, and face her

reverse
- when he pulls away, step back
- he pulls you to his left side
- he places your L hand on out-side of his R waist and your R hand palm out on outside of your R waist

shuffle
- moving forward, turn counter-clockwise

release
- when he drops your L hand and pulls you at right waist, turn left 1 turn

- he takes your L hand and then your R hand, and you face him

Pull her at the waist. *To release, pull her firmly with your left hand.*

. . . and spin away. *Spin in opposite directions, man to the right, woman to the left.*

Turn back and take her hand. *Normally your right hand takes her left hand first.*

. . . and return to basic step. *Then you face each other, holding both hands.*

Over the Shoulder

Facing each other, the man and woman turn slightly left and raise both hands over their heads. They place their right hands behind each other's neck. Then they release their left hands, pass them in front of their waists and between their bodies, and hold hands. After a few turns to the right, they drop their left hands (placing them behind their backs) and slide their right hands down each other's arms until they hold hands. As he dances toward her, he lifts his right hand, and she turns left under it, as they exchange places. Then he changes hands behind his back. As he dances toward her a second time, he lifts his left hand, and she turns left under it, as they exchange places.

Man

start
- hold both hands
- turn left ¼, raising hands over head
- R hand behind her neck
- L hand between bodies, holding her hand

shuffle
- moving forward, turn clockwise

Woman

start
- hold both hands
- turn left ¼, raising hands over head
- R hand behind his neck
- L hand between bodies, holding his hand

shuffle
- moving forward, turn clockwise

Raise hands. *Start by raising both hands above head level, turning slightly left.*

. . . drop right hands on shoulders. *Men, lower your hand gently on her shoulder, behind her neck. You don't need to press her behind the back to make her go faster. Ladies, your hand goes on his shoulder.*

. . . and hold left hands. *Pass your left hand between the two bodies at the waist, and hold hands. Ladies, your left hand goes in front, not behind your back.*

Turn clockwise. *Keep your arms straight, so there's space between you.*

Release left hands. *And place them behind your backs.*

. . . slide right hands down arms. *Moving apart, with arms straight, slide right hands down each other's arm, until you hold hands.*

. . . and turn her under your arm. *Dance forward to your left, turning her under your right arm.*

Change hands behind your back. *As you step past her, place her right hand in your left hand, behind your back.*

. . . and pull away. *As you pull away from her, turn left to face her.*

release
- drop L hand and place it behind back
- move away and slide R hand down her arm
- hold R hands
- step forward to left and turn her under R hand (as you exchange places)
- change hands behind back and turn left $1/2$

Raise your left hand. *As you dance toward her a second time, raise your left hand.*

release
- when he drops your L hand, place it behind your back
- move away and slide R hand down his arm
- hold R hands
- when he steps to your right, turn left $1/2$ under his R hand (as you exchange places)
- he changes hands

. . . and turn her. *Ladies, turn left under his raised hand. Men, turn right to face her.*

Back to normal position. *Now you face each other, hold both hands, and get ready for the next move.*

• raise L hand and turn right ½, turning her to your right side (as you exchange places)

• when he raises your R hand, turn left ½ under his L hand (as you exchange places)

Bend and Turn

After dropping his right hand, the man takes the woman's right hand with his right hand. Holding his left hand at his side, he makes half a turn left to nestle at her right side. He slides his left hand under her right arm and takes her left hand behind her back. Now they are facing in the same direction and holding hands behind their backs. They shuffle back and then forward. As they reach the farthest point forward, they pause and bend forward slightly and turn away from each other to face in the opposite direction. They shuffle forward, changing direction as before. To release, they drop both hands and face each other. If she has been on his left side, with his left hand he takes her right hand and turns her on his right side. If she has been on his right side, with his right hand he takes her left hand and turns her on his left side.

Drop your right hand. *Men, to start the move, step back and free your right hand. Then take her right hand with your right hand.*

. . . start turning left. *As you turn against her right arm, hold your left hand at your side. Ladies, start moving back.*

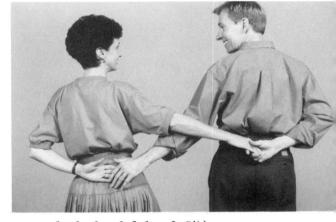

. . . and take her left hand. *Slide your left hand across her back and take her left hand, palm out.*

Man

start
- R hand take her R hand
- turn right, with your L hand at your side, and slide your L hand under her R arm
- take her L hand behind back

Woman

start
- he takes your R hand
- when he turns right, with his L hand at his side, and slides his L hand under your R arm, take his L hand behind back

shuffle
• shuffle back and forward

reverse
• bending forward slightly, turn outward and reverse direction

shuffle
• shuffle forward
• reverse as before

release
• drop both hands
• use one of two releases:

shuffle
• shuffle back and forward

reverse
• bending forward slightly, turn outward and reverse direction

shuffle
• shuffle forward
• reverse as before

release
• he drops both hands
• use one of two releases:

Shuffle back, then forward. *As you shuffle, you hold both hands behind your backs in a handshake with thumbs interlocked.*

Bend and turn. *When you're ready to turn, gently squeeze her hands. Both bend slightly forward and turn outward and around.*

Shuffle forward. *When you shuffle, keep your bodies erect; don't bend over.*

Bend and turn. *Men, when you reach the farthest point forward, pause and bend. Ladies, bend and turn with him.*

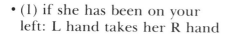

- (1) if she has been on your left: L hand takes her R hand

- raise L hand and turn right ¹/₂, turning her to your right side
- (2) if she has been on your right: R hand takes her L hand
- raise R hand and turn left ¹/₂, turning her to your left side

- (1) if he has been on your right: his L hand takes your R hand
- when he raises your R hand, turn left ¹/₂

- (2) if he has been on your left: his R hand takes your L hand
- when he raises your L hand, turn right ¹/₂

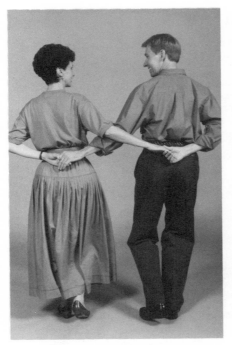

Shuffle forward. *The final shuffle leads to the release. The release will begin when the man drops both hands.*

Lift her hand. *Your left hand takes her right hand, and she begins to turn to the left.*

. . . and she emerges from a turn. *Ladies, you complete the turn and face him.*

Back to normal. *Hold hands, and you're ready for the next move.*

The next three swing moves (turns and spins) are often used as transitional or resting steps.

Simple Turns

The man drops his right hand. Raising his left hand, he steps forward to his right and then turns left, while the woman turns right ½ under his left arm. Turning right, he pulls the woman back, and she turns left ½ under his arm. They end facing each other.

Man	**Woman**
• drop R hand and raise L hand	• he drops your L hand and raises your R hand
• step forward to right, turning left ½	• when he steps to your left, turn right ½ under his arm
• pull her back, turning right ½, and face her	• turn left ½ under his arm and face him

Fig. 1   Fig. 2   Fig. 3

Fig. 1. Double: first turn. *Men, step forward to right, raising your left hand. Ladies, turn right under his arm.*

Fig. 2. Double: rock back. *Both partners fall back at arm's length.*

Fig. 3. Double: second turn. *Ladies, turn left under his arm.*

Combination Turns

The man drops his right hand. Raising his left hand, he steps forward to his left, and the woman turns left ½ under his arm. Then he turns left ½ under his own arm. They end facing each other.

Man

• drop R hand and raise L hand

• step forward to left

• after she turns under your arm, turn left ½ under your arm and face her

Woman

• he drops your L hand and raises your R hand

• when he steps to your right, turn left ½ under his arm and face him

Combination: first turn. *Men, step forward to left, raising your left hand. Ladies, turn left under his arm.*

Combination: second turn. *Men, as she finishes her turn, you start to turn.*

Combination: end. *And you turn left under your arm.*

Spins

The man drops his right hand. Raising his left hand, he allows the woman to hold his fingers lightly. She spins left several times, or until he lowers his hand (or she squeezes his hand).

Man

• drop R hand and raise L hand
• she spins left several times
• to stop her, lower L hand

Woman

• he raises your R hand
• spin left several times
• to stop him, squeeze his hand

Spins: start. *Raise your left hand over her head, and she starts to spin left.*

Spins: middle. *Ladies, spin left as long as his hand is up. Look at your partner at the end of each spin. If you want to stop, squeeze his hand.*

Spins: end. *Men, lower your left hand to end the spins.*

The next three swing moves (two versions of Behind the Back, and Reverse Side-by-Side) begin in the same way. The couple face each other and hold hands directly across (as in the beginner steps). The man raises his right hand, starting the woman in a left turn.

Behind the Back (1)

The man raises his right hand and, turning slightly right, turns the woman left until she faces behind him. At the same time he places his right hand (and her left hand) behind his neck. Their other hands pass behind her back. They turn counterclockwise, keeping their left arms straight. To reverse, he moves left and slides her to his right side, behind his back. Their hands rest behind each other's back. They turn clockwise, keeping their right arms straight. To release, he drops his right hand, steps back, and turns her on his right side.

Man

start

- lift R hand, lowering L hand, and turn right ¼ to face in opposite directions

- place R hand behind your neck and L hand behind her back

Woman

start

- he lifts your L hand, lowering your R hand, and turns you left ¾ to face in opposite directions

- he places your L hand behind his neck and R hand behind your back

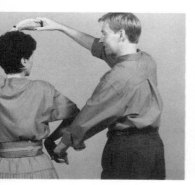  

Fig. 1   **Fig. 2**   **Fig. 3**

Fig. 1. Raise her left hand. *The next three swing moves all begin the same way: the man raises the woman's left hand.*

Fig. 2. She turns left. *Ladies, whenever he raises your left hand, turn left as far as you can go.*

Fig. 3. In position. *Men, be decisive and show her what to do next. Lower your right hand either behind your neck (this dance) or in front of it (the next dance). Ladies, place your right hand palm out behind your back, your left hand palm out against the back of his neck.*

Both turn left. *Keep your left arms straight. Leave some space between you.*

She slides right. *Move left, lowering your right hand and sliding her behind you to your right side.*

Hands on hips. *Both partners place their left hands palm out behind their backs.*

Both turn right. *As you turn, look at each other across your shoulders.*

shuffle
- moving forward, with left arms straight, turn counter-clockwise

reverse
- move left and slide her behind your back to right side to face in opposite directions

- place L hand behind your back, palm out, and R hand behind her back

shuffle
- moving forward, with right arms straight, turn clockwise

release
- drop R hand and step back
- raise L hand and turn her to your right

shuffle
- moving forward, with left arms straight, turn counter-clockwise

reverse
- he moves left and slides you behind his back to his right side to face in opposite directions

- he places your R hand behind his back, and L hand behind your back, palm out

shuffle
- moving forward, with right arms straight, turn clockwise

release
- he drops your L hand, raises your R hand, and turns you left $1/2$

Start of release. *Men, drop your right hand and step back, turning left.*

She turns left. *Ladies, turn left under his left arm and end by facing him.*

Behind the Back (2)

The step begins in the same way, except that the man places his right hand (and her left hand) in front of his neck. They turn counterclockwise, keeping their left arms straight. To reverse, he lifts his right hand and then his left, while she makes one and a half turns right, ending at his right side. They turn clockwise, keeping their right arms straight. To release, he drops his right hand, steps back, and turns her on his right side.

Man	**Woman**
start	*start*
• lift R hand, lowering L hand, and turn right ¹/₄ to face in opposite directions	• he lifts your L hand, lowering your R hand, and turns you left ³/₄ to face in opposite directions

Raise her left hand. *These three steps all begin the same way: the man raises the lady's left hand.*

She turns left. *Ladies, whenever he raises your left hand, turn left as far as you can go.*

Drop her hand in front. *Men, place your right hand palm out in front of your neck.*

In position. *Ladies, place your right hand palm out behind your back.*

- place R hand in front of your neck, and L hand behind her back

shuffle
- moving forward, with left arms straight, turn counter-clockwise

reverse
- lift R hand, then L hand, and turn left ½ to face in opposite directions

- place L hand in front of your neck, and R hand behind her back

shuffle
- moving forward with right arms straight, turn clockwise

- he places your L hand in front of his neck, and R hand behind your back, palm out

shuffle
- moving forward, with left arms straight, turn counter-clockwise

reverse
- he lifts your L hand, then your R hand, and turns you right 1½ turns to face in opposite directions
- he places your R hand in front of his neck, and L hand behind your back, palm out

shuffle
- moving forward with right arms straight, turn clockwise

Both turn left. *Keep your left arms straight. Leave some space between you.*

release
- drop R hand and step back
- raise L hand and turn her to your right

release
- he drops your L hand, raises your R hand, and turns you left $1/2$

Start of reverse. *Men, raise your right hand and start her in a right turn. Step back and turn slightly to the left.*

Turning into position. *Ladies, turn completely around to the right. Settle into the opposite position.*

In position. *Men, place your left hand palm out in front of your neck. Ladies, place your left hand palm out behind your back.*

Both turn right. *As always, look into each other's eyes and smile.*

Start of release. *Men, drop your right hand and step back.*

Raise left hand. *Raise your left hand and begin turning her.*

She turns left. *Ladies, turn left under his left arm and end by facing him.*

Reverse Side-by-Side

The man raises his right hand, turning left, and the woman turns left in almost a full circle. They face the same direction, touching shoulders. They hold inside forearms upright. His left arm passes in front of his waist, and her right arm passes behind her back. To reverse direction, he raises his right hand, turning right, and turns her right in half a circle. To release, either (1) he raises his left hand and turns her left to face him or (2) he drops his right hand and turns her to his right.

Raise her left hand. *All three steps start in the same way, turning the lady to the left. Men, be decisive about what happens next.*

Lower her left hand. *Men, drop your right hand (holding her left hand) between your bodies.*

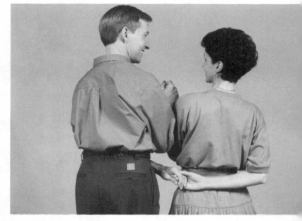

Hand behind the back. *Ladies, your right arm passes behind your back.*

Shuffle back and forward. *When shuffling, press your shoulders together.*

Man

start
- raise R hand and turn left $^1/_4$

- pull R hand in and raise forearm
- rest R elbow on your L hand

shuffle
- shuffle back and forward

reverse
- raise R hand and turn right $^1/_2$

- raise L hand over her head

- pull L hand in and raise forearm
- rest L elbow on your R hand

Woman

start
- when he raises your L hand, turn left $^3/_4$
- he pulls your L hand in and raises your forearm
- you rest L elbow on your R hand

shuffle
- shuffle back and forward

reverse
- when he raises your L hand, turn right $^1/_2$
- he raises your R hand over your head
- he pulls your R hand in and raises your forearm
- rest R elbow on your L hand

Start of reverse. *Men, raise your right hand again, and both of you turn around to the right.*

Lower her right hand. *Men, drop your left hand (holding her right hand) between your bodies.*

Shuffle forward. *You may look at each other or straight forward.*

shuffle
• shuffle forward

release
• two alternatives:

• (1) raise L hand and turn left ¼ to face her

shuffle
• shuffle forward

release
• two alternatives:

• (1) when he raises your R hand, turn left ¾ to face him

First release (1). *Men, there are two ways to release her. The first is to raise your left hand and turn her to the left again.*

First release (2). *Ladies, you end by facing him.*

Second release (1). *Men, drop your right hand and turn her to your right.*

Second release (2). *Ladies, turn left and end facing him.*

- (2) drop R hand and step back
- raise L hand and turn her to your right

- (2) he drops your L hand, raises your R hand, and turns you left $1/2$

The next group of swing moves (Crossed-Hands Turn with Windmill, Julie Turn, Little Window, Big Window, and Tunnel) all begin in the same way. The man and woman cross hands, left over right.

Crossed-Hands Turn

The step begins with two crossed-hands turns by the woman which evolve into two windmill turns by both partners.

They cross hands, left over right. By raising his left hand and lowering his right hand, he starts her in a full left turn. Then, raising his right and left hands alternately over his head (and lowering the other hands), he turns her first left and then right, twice each, in complete turns. The move evolves into the windmill (see below).

Man

start
- cross hands L over R
- while facing her, raise L hand, lowering R hand, and start her into left turn

Woman

start
- cross hands L over R
- while facing you, he raises your L hand, lowering your R hand, and starts you into left turn

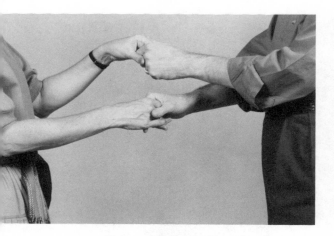

Crossed hands. *Six swing moves start with left hands crossed over right hands.*

Raise left hands. *Men, when you raise your left hand, open your palm and rotate your hand, thumb down.*

. . . lower right hands. *This starts her into a left turn. Be decisive and show her what to do next.*

. . . and she turns left. *Ladies, whenever he raises your left hand, turn left.*

Raise right hands. *Ladies, each time you make a complete turn to face him, pausing briefly.*

. . . and she turns right. *Men, by raising right and left hands alternately, you turn her back and forth. Pause briefly after each turn, before turning her the other way.*

- raise R hand, lowering L, turning her left
- raise L hand, lowering R, turning her right
- repeat both moves
- as you start her in third left turn, continue into windmill

- as he raises your R hand, he turns you left
- as he raises your L hand, he turns you right
- he repeats both moves
- as he turns you left again, continue into windmill

Windmill

Continuing with crossed-hands turns, he raises his right hand and starts her in a third left turn. At the same time he turns right and away from her for two full turns. When he sees the back of her head the second time, he places his right hand (and her right hand) on her right shoulder. They shuffle back and forward, reverse direction (turning around so that she is on his left), and shuffle forward. To release, he drops his left hand from her left shoulder and turns her to the left with his right hand. He places her right hand in his left hand, and they hold both hands.

Continue into the windmill. *As she starts the third left turn, the move evolves into the windmill.*

He turns right. *As both of you turn, she looks at the back of your head.*

. . . and she turns left. *And you look at the back of her head.*

End of the fourth turn. *The second time you see the back of her head, lower your right hand on her shoulder.*

Man

start

- as you start her in third left turn, raise R hand, lowering L, then L hand, lowering R, while turning right
- you make two right turns in a circular motion until you see back of her head the second time
- place R hand on her right shoulder, and L hand in front of you

shuffle

- shuffle back and forward

reverse

- turn around to right to reverse direction

Woman

start

- he starts you left again, raising your R hand, lowering L, then L hand, lowering R, while you turn left
- you make two left turns in a circular motion until he faces you from behind the second time
- he places your R hand on your right shoulder, and holds your L hand in front

shuffle

- shuffle back and forward

reverse

- he turns you around to right to reverse direction

Shuffle back and forth. *This is known as the varsovienne position (from a nineteenth-century dance).*

. . . and turn around. *To reverse, simply turn toward her and around, turning her with you.*

Shuffle some more. *As your hand settles on her shoulder, start moving forward.*

He drops his left hand. *To release, drop the hand on her shoulder and raise the other hand.*

. . . and she turns. *Ladies, turn to the left to face him.*

• you are on her right side with L hand on her left shoulder and R hand in front of you

shuffle
• shuffle forward

release
• drop L hand from her left shoulder
• with R hand turn her to left

• he is on your right side with your L hand on your left shoulder and your R hand in front of him

shuffle
• shuffle forward

release
• he drops your L hand from your left shoulder
• you turn to left

Julie Turn

With hands crossed (left over right), the man raises his left hand and lowers his right hand. The woman turns left $1\frac{1}{4}$ and the man left $\frac{1}{4}$. They face in opposite directions, right sides touching. Their left arms arch over their heads. His right arm crosses in front of her waist, her right arm behind her back, with hands on her left side. They shuffle clockwise. To reverse, he lowers his left hand and raises his right hand, turning right $\frac{1}{2}$ as she turns right $1\frac{1}{2}$. Their left sides touch. They arch their right hands over their heads. His left arm crosses in front of her waist, her left arm behind her back, with hands on her right side. They shuffle counterclockwise. To release, with his left hand he pulls her waist and spins her left $1\frac{1}{4}$ beneath their right hands, to face him.

Crossed hands. *Five swing moves start with left hands crossed over right hands.*

Raise left hands. *Men, when you raise your left hand, open your palm and rotate your hand, thumb down. This time keep your right hand down.*

. . . and she turns left. *Ladies, whenever he raises your left hand, turn left as far as you can go.*

Man

start
- cross hands L over R
- raise L hand and lower R hand, turning left ¼
- using L hand, guide her through left turn until right side touches her
- arch L hand over her head
- R arm across her waist and R hand on her left side

shuffle
- moving forward, turn clockwise

Woman

start
- cross hands L over R
- he raises L hand and lowers R hand
- with his L hand, he guides you as you turn left 1¼ until right side touches him
- arch L hand over his head
- R arm behind your waist and R hand on your left side

shuffle
- moving forward, turn clockwise

Turn clockwise. *When you turn, touch fingertips or open palms. Don't grip each other's hands.*

Step back. *Men, when you start to change direction, step back slightly.*

. . . and raise your right hand. *In changing direction, his arms swing down and across her back as she turns right. He waits until he sees her back.*

Turn counterclockwise. *Stand erect and pivot on your inside foot.*

reverse
- lower L hand and raise R hand, turning right ¹/₂
- using R hand, guide her through right turn until left side touches her
- arch R hand over her head
- L arm in front of her waist and L hand on her right side

shuffle
- moving forward, turn counter-clockwise

release
- with your L hand, pull her waist and spin her out to face you

reverse
- he lowers L hand and raises R hand
- with his R hand, he guides you as you turn right 1¹/₂ until left side touches him
- arch R hand over his head
- L arm behind your waist and L hand on your right side

shuffle
- moving forward, turn counter-clockwise

release
- he frees your L hand at waist and turns you left 1¹/₄ to face him

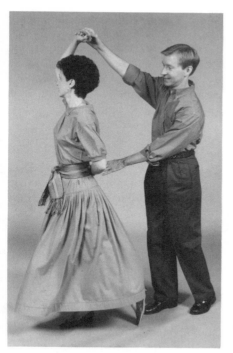

He pulls her waist. *To release her, step back and pull her waist with your left hand. Ladies, spin to the left.*

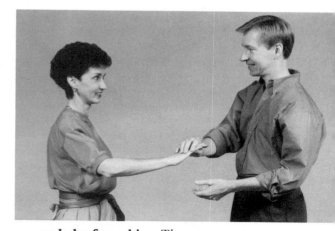

. . . and she faces him. *The woman ends in the normal position, facing the man.*

Little Window

With hands crossed (left over right), the man raises both hands over their heads and lets his middle fingers dangle loosely. The woman lightly holds the middle finger of each hand and turns left 1¾ times. Their right hands end up joined through a window formed by their left arms, elbows, and raised hands. They shuffle counterclockwise. To reverse, he raises both hands over their heads, in the same way, and she turns right 2½ times. Their left hands end up joined through a window formed by their right arms, elbows, and raised hands. They shuffle clockwise. To release, he raises both hands, she turns left to face him, and they end up with crossed hands.

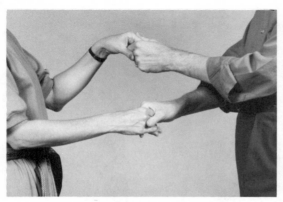

Crossed hands. *Five swing moves begin with left hands crossed over right hands.*

Raise both hands. *Men, hold your fingers above her head. Let the middle finger on each hand dangle loosely.*

. . . and she turns left. *Men, keep your hands apart (so they don't get tangled as she turns). As she turns left, count one and two.*

Settling into a window. *Ladies, when you reach the end of your turns lower your right hand.*

Man

start
- cross hands L over R
- raise both hands over head and dangle middle fingers
- she holds the middle finger of each hand and turns left
- after she turns left 1¾ times, lower hands and turn right ¼, bringing your right hand to rest on your upper left arm
- hold L arm against her arm, with forearm up and R hand through window

shuffle
- moving forward, turn counter-clockwise

Woman

start
- cross hands L over R
- he raises both hands over head
- grasp middle finger of each hand and start to turn left
- after you turn left 1¾ times, lower hands, bringing your right hand to rest on your up-per left arm
- hold L arm against his arm, with forearm up and R hand through window

shuffle
- moving forward, turn counter-clockwise

Shuffle counterclockwise. *Look through the little window and smile.*

Raise both hands again. *Men, help her by counting as she turns, every time she faces you. As she turns right, count one, two, three.*

. . . and she settles into a window. *Ladies, as you turn, spot his face and count. Bring your left hand down.*

reverse
- raise both hands over head and dangle middle fingers
- she holds the middle finger of each hand and turns right
- after she turns right 2½ times, lower hands and turn left ½, bringing your left hand to rest on your upper right arm
- hold R arm against her arm, with forearm up and L hand through window

shuffle
- moving forward, turn clockwise

release
- raise both hands over head and dangle middle fingers
- she holds the middle finger of each hand and turns left
- after she turns left ¾ to face you, lower hands crossed L over R

reverse
- he raises both hands over head
- grasp middle finger of each hand and start to turn right
- after you turn right 2½ times, lower hands, bringing your left hand to rest on your upper right arm
- hold R arm against his arm, with forearm up and L hand through window

shuffle
- moving forward, turn clockwise

release
- he raises both hands over head
- grasp middle finger of each hand and start to turn left
- after you turn left ¾ to face him, he lowers your hands crossed L over R

Shuffle clockwise. *The upper part of your arms, from shoulder to elbow, should touch each other.*

She turns left. *Ladies, to end the move, you turn around to the left.*

. . . and you face each other. *Both of you return to crossed hands.*

Big Window

With hands crossed (left over right), the man raises first his left and then his right hand (lowering the left hand) and turns the woman left 1¾, while he turns right ¼. They arch their right hands over their heads to form a big window. Their left hands pass behind her back to rest on her right side. They shuffle counterclockwise. To reverse, he raises his left hand and lowers his right hand and turns her right 1½, while he turns left ½. They arch their left hands over their heads. Their right hands pass behind her back to rest on her left side. They shuffle clockwise. To release, he lowers her left hand, and she spins left ¾ to face him.

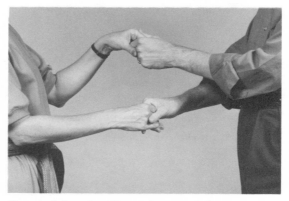

Crossed hands. *Five swing moves begin with left hands crossed over right hands.*

He raises left hand. *Ladies, when he raises your left hand, start a turn to the left, as far as you can go.*

. . . and then right hands. *Men, when you see her back, swing your arms across, lowering your left hand and raising your right hand.*

Turn counterclockwise. *When you turn, touch finger tips or open palms. Don't grip each other's hands.*

Man

start
- cross hands L over R
- raise L hand, starting her in left turn
- then raise R hand, lowering L, and turn her left 1¾ while you turn right ¼
- arch R hand over head to form big window

shuffle
- moving forward, turn counter-clockwise

reverse
- raise L hand, lowering R, and turn her right 1½ while you turn left ½

Woman

start
- cross hands L over R
- he raises L hand, starting you in left turn
- he raises R hand, lowering L, and turns you left 1¾ while he turns right ¼
- arch R hand over head to form big window

shuffle
- moving forward, turn counter-clockwise

reverse
- he raises L hand, lowering R, and turns you right 1½ while he turns left ½

Raise left hands. *Men, when you start to change direction, step back slightly.*

. . . and she turns right. *Men, in changing direction, your arms swing down and across her back as she turns right. Wait until you see her back.*

Turn clockwise. *Stand erect and pivot on your inside foot.*

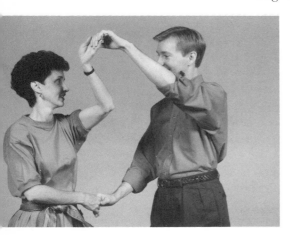

Step back. *Men, to begin the release, lower your left hand and pull her with your right hand into a left turn.*

. . . and she ends facing him. *You can also go straight from the big window into the little window. Men, just raise both hands above your heads and dangle fingers, while she keeps turning left.*

• arch L hand over head to form big window

shuffle
• moving forward, turn clockwise

release
• lower L hand and pull her with R hand to face her

• arch L hand over head to form big window

shuffle
• moving forward, turn clockwise

release
• he lowers your L hand and spins you left ³/₄ to face him

Tunnel

With hands crossed (left over right), the man lowers his right hand and raises his left hand (then passing it over his head). He uses his left hand to guide her around his back and to his left side. The woman, dancing around him, passes his right side, back, and left side. He arches his left elbow, making a hole, and she bends and ducks through that tunnel. He arches his right elbow, making a hole, and she backs through that tunnel. She turns right and faces in the same direction as him, on his right side. They shuffle back and forward. To reverse, he turns her to face him, makes a hole with first his right elbow, which she ducks through, and then his left elbow, which she backs through. She turns left and faces in the same direction as him, on his left side. They shuffle back and forward. To release, he drops both her hands and steps away.

Man

start
- cross hands L over R
- raise L hand, lowering R
- pass L hand over your head to guide her around your back, holding R hand behind waist
- when she reaches left side, lower L hand on your left and raise L elbow to form hole
- when she passes around back, raise R elbow to form hole
- turn her to right

Woman

start
- cross hands L over R
- he raises L hand, lowering R, and uses his L hand to guide you around his back, starting on his right side
- when you reach his left side, turn right, duck through hole, and pass around his back

- back through hole on right and turn to right

Guide her around back. *Men, raise your left hand and pull her toward your right side and behind you to your left side.*

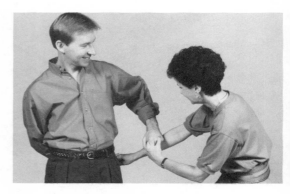

Make hole with elbow. *The hole has to be big enough for her to get through.*

Duck through left hole. *Ladies, bend over when you duck under his arm. It's undignified but fun.*

Back through right hole. *And bend when you back out, no matter what anyone thinks.*

She turns slightly right. *Men, use your arms to turn her so that you are side by side.*

Shuffle. *Keep together as you dance back and forth.*

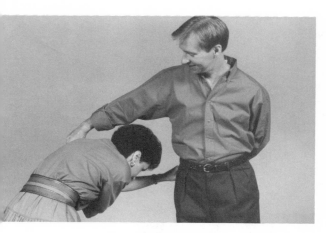

Make hole with elbow. *The hole has to be big enough for her to get through.*

Duck through right hole. *Ladies, bend from the waist when you duck.*

Back through left hole. *And bend from the waist when you back up.*

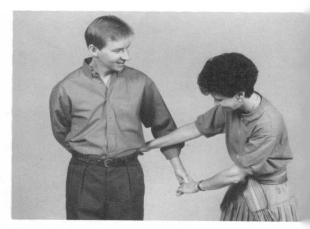

She turns slightly left. *Men, use your arms to turn her so that you are side by side.*

shuffle
• shuffle back and forward

reverse
• turn her left to face you
• raise R elbow to form hole

• when she passes around back, raise L elbow to form hole
• turn her to left

shuffle
• shuffle back and forth

release
• release her hands and step away

shuffle
• shuffle back and forward

reverse
• he turns you left to face him

• duck through hole and pass around his back
• back through hole on his left and turn to left

shuffle
• shuffle back and forth

release
• he releases your hands and steps away

Release. *Men, drop both her hands as you step away, then take her right hand.*

Shuffle. *Look at each other as you shuffle.*

The next four swing moves (Sweetheart Chain, Pretzel, Reverse Pretzel, and Crawfish) all involve the familiar sweetheart position. Together with the original Sweetheart, they can be used in a variety of combinations.

Sweetheart Chain

The man wraps the woman in the sweetheart position on his right side. Alternating dropping her left and right hands, and taking them up again, he circles her clockwise, while she circles him clockwise, both facing in the same direction. To reverse, he moves her to the sweetheart position on his left side. Alternating dropping her right and left hands, and taking them up again, he circles her counterclockwise, while she circles him counterclockwise, both facing in the same direction. To release, he takes her in either the sweetheart position or the reverse sweetheart position, on either his right or his left side, and they turn. He drops his hand in front of them. If his arm is behind her (the sweetheart position), he spins her out to right or left. If her arm is behind him (the reverse sweetheart position), he spins out to right or left.

Sweetheart position. *You may start from either side. Here the woman is on the right.*

He drops his right hand. *Start by moving around each other in a clockwise direction. Always keep your free hand above your partner's arm.*

. . . and he slides right in front of her. *Both partners circle each other (not just the woman circling the man).*

He drops his left hand. *As you circle each other, remain in a fixed position, relative to some object or person across the room.*

. . . and he slides left behind her. *Men, raise your left hand across her left shoulder, then drop it again.*

Take her hand again. *Completing each circle, briefly hold hands in the sweetheart position.*

Man

start
- sweetheart position (on left)

shuffle
- drop your R hand
- as you slide to right in front of her, bring R hand above L arm and take her L hand
- drop your L hand
- as you slide to left behind her, bring L hand across and take her R hand

- (do this several times)

reverse (optional)
- shift her to left side

shuffle (optional)
- drop your L hand

Woman

start
- sweetheart position (on right)

shuffle
- he drops your L hand
- as you slide to left behind him, take his R hand

- he drops your R hand
- as you slide to right in front of him, take his L hand, bringing your R hand over your L

- (do this several times)

reverse (optional)
- he shifts you to left side

shuffle (optional)
- he drops your R hand

Sweetheart on the other side. *The chain may also start with the woman on the left, or she may shift to the left during the dance.*

He drops his left hand. *This time slide around each other in a counter-clockwise direction.*

. . . drops his right hand. *Remember to fix your movement relative to some object or person across the room.*

. . . and slides right behind of her. *As you circle, don't twist your bodies; keep them straight.*

Take her hand again. *Completing each circle, briefly hold hands in the sweetheart position.*

- as you slide to left in front of her, bring L hand above R arm and take her R hand
- drop your R hand
- as you slide to right behind her, bring R hand across and take her L hand
- (do this several times)

release
- sweetheart or reverse sweet-heart release

- as you slide to right behind him, take his L hand

- he drops your L hand
- as you slide to left in front of him, take his R hand, bringing your L hand over your R
- (do this several times)

release
- sweetheart or reverse sweet-heart release

The man releases the woman in one of four ways:

1. If your arm is behind her, and she is on your right, spin her out to the right.

2. If your arm is behind her, and she is on your left, spin her out to the left.

3. If her arm is behind you, and you are on the right, spin out to the right.

4. If her arm is behind you, and you are on the left, spin out to the left.

Pretzel

They face each other, holding hands. Stepping back, the man drops his right hand and places it behind his back. As he dances toward the woman, he lifts his left hand. As he passes her, he takes her left hand with his right hand. She moves behind his back. He shifts her to his right side, raising his right hand and lowering his left hand, with arms straight. Turning slightly right to face her, he rolls his right hand in a circle, starting up, back, and around. This turns her right $\frac{1}{2}$. During this movement, he turns left $\frac{1}{2}$, while she turns left $\frac{1}{2}$. He raises his left hand over her head, rests his right hand on the right side of her waist, and lowers his left arm in front of her, in the sweetheart position. They shuffle in the sweetheart position and release as usual.

Man

start
- hold both hands
- step back and drop R hand behind back
- dancing toward her, raise L hand

Woman

start
- hold both hands
- he steps back and drops your L hand
- as he dances toward you, he raises his L hand

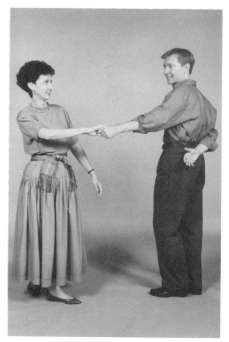

To start, step back. *Men, drop your right hand and place it behind your back.*

. . . offer her your hand. *Now dance toward her, lifting your left hand.*

. . . and shift her behind your back. *Keep your right arm straight when you turn away from her and slide her to your right.*

Turn to face each other. *Men, turn slightly right. Ladies, turn slightly right.*

Quickly, roll your hand. *What happens next is almost too quick to describe. Ladies, bend forward as the move starts.*

. . . turn left and carry her hand over your head. *While the man turns left, the woman turns first right and then left.*

. . . and lower your right hand. *Now you both are facing in the same direction.*

. . . and your left hand. *The move begins to look familiar.*

. . . into the sweetheart position.
Surprise!

- as you pass her, take her L hand with your R hand
- she moves behind your back
- sliding to left, shift her to right side, raising R hand and lowering L

- turn slightly right to face her
- roll R hand in a circle up, back, down, forward near your face
- turn left ½
- raise your L hand over her head, rest your R hand on her right waist, and lower your L hand in front of her in sweetheart position

shuffle
- sweetheart moves

release
- sweetheart release or reverse pretzel (below)

- as he passes you, he takes your L hand with his R hand
- move around his back
- as he slides to left, he shifts you to your left (his right side), raising your L hand and lowering R

- turn slightly right to face him
- he rolls your L hand over your head, turning you right ½
- he turns you left ½
- he raises your R hand over your head, rests his R hand on your right waist, and lowers your R hand in front in sweetheart position

shuffle
- sweetheart moves

release
- sweetheart release or reverse pretzel (below)

Reverse Pretzel

They finish the pretzel in the sweetheart position. He raises his left hand and lowers his right hand, turning her right $1/2$ to face him. Then he turns left $1/2$, and she turns right $1/2$. He shifts her to his right side, lowering his left hand and raising his right hand above her head. They perform the pretzel again and end in the sweetheart position.

Man

- pretzel
- sweetheart position

start

- raise L hand and lower R hand, turning her right to face you

Woman

- pretzel
- sweetheart position

start

- he raises your R hand and lowers your L hand, turning you right $1/2$ to face him

Starting the reverse. *Men, raise your left hand and lower your right. This turns her to face you.*

Back to back. *Then turn left. This turns her right, so that you are back to back.*

Reverse hands. *As you raise your right hand and lower your left, you shift her to the right. Now you are starting the pretzel again.*

- turn left ½, turning her right ½ back to back
- lower L hand and raise R hand
- continue with pretzel (above)
- sweetheart shuffle and release

- when he turns left ½, turn right ½ back to back
- he lowers your R hand and raises your L hand
- continue with pretzel (above)
- sweetheart shuffle and release

Crawfish

They start in the sweetheart position. He raises his right elbow, and she backs under it. As she raises her right arm and his left arm, he turns right to face her and bends, ducks under her raised arm, and turns right ½. Now she has him in a sweetheart position, behind him and to his right. They shuffle back and forward. He backs under her left arm (and his left arm) and turns her left into the sweetheart position.

Man

start
- sweetheart position
- when you raise R elbow, she backs under it
- when she raises her R arm, turn right to face her and bend
- duck under the raised arm and turn right ½
- she now holds you in sweetheart position behind you and to right

shuffle
- shuffle back and forward

release
- back under her L arm and turn her left into sweetheart position

Woman

start
- sweetheart position
- when he raises R elbow, back under his R arm
- when you raise R arm, he turns right to face you

- he ducks under your R arm and turns right ½
- you now hold him in sweetheart position behind him and to his right

shuffle
- shuffle back and forward

release
- he backs under your L arm and turns you left into sweetheart position

Sweetheart. *You start in the familiar sweetheart position, the woman on the right.*

She backs up. *Men, raise your right elbow. Ladies, back under it.*

. . . he ducks through. *Men, turn right and duck under her right elbow.*

. . . and she holds him. *Now she holds you in the sweetheart position, on her left, and you shuffle (or go straight to the release).*

He backs out. *To release, back out under her left arm.*

. . . and turns her into a sweet-heart. *Ladies, turn left into the normal sweetheart position.*

St. Charles

The final move is lagniappe—a gift for the dancer whose mind goes blank and forgets all the steps learned so far. The St. Charles streetcar in New Orleans follows a similar route around a semicircle and back.

They start by holding hands. He raises both hands to his right and, passing them over his head and behind to his left, leads her clockwise around him. When she reaches his left side, he drops his right hand, then holds both hands when she faces him. To reverse, he raises both hands and, passing them over his head and behind to his right, leads her counterclockwise around him. When she reaches his right side, he drops his left hand, then holds both hands when she faces him.

Fig. 1   **Fig. 2**   **Fig. 3**

Fig. 1. He raises hands to right. *Men, raise higher the hand you're leading her with.*

Fig. 2. . . . guides her around back. *Pass your hands over your head and to the side.*

Fig. 3. . . . and releases her. *When she reaches the other side, lower your hand into a little window. Then release her hand.*

Man

start

- hold both hands
- raise both hands to right

- pass them over your head and behind to left side, leading her clockwise
- when she is on your left, drop right hand
- when she faces you, hold both hands

Woman

start

- hold both hands
- he raises both hands to his right
- he passes them over his head and behind to his left side
- follow clockwise
- when you are on his left, he drops your left hand
- when you face him, hold both hands

Fig. 4   **Fig. 5**   **Fig. 6**

Fig. 4. He raises hands to left. *Men, raise higher the hand you're leading her with.*

Fig. 5. . . . guides her around back. *Pass your hands over your head and to the side.*

Fig. 6. . . . and releases her. *When she reaches the other side, lower your hand into a little window. Then release her hand.*

reverse
- raise both hands to left
- pass them over your head and behind to right side, leading her counterclockwise
- when she is on your right, drop left hand
- when she faces you, hold both hands

reverse
- he raises both hands to his left
- he passes them over his head and behind to his right side
- follow counterclockwise
- when you are on his right, he drops your right hand
- when you face him, hold both hands

III. Dances for Small Groups

Troika

Normally in this dance a man dances with two women. (If there are three women, one takes the role of the man.) He leads them through several moves, calling out each move and giving directions. (Here we list seven moves, not necessarily danced in the order given.) They dance the shuffle to a two-step tune.

(1) Pattycake
- The man is in the middle, with the women on both sides.
- He pulls the women close in the side-by-side position, and they shuffle back and forward. (While shuffling, each woman lifts the hem of her skirt or places her free hand behind her back.)
- He extends his arms and leads the women toward each other. They pat their free hands.
- He pulls the women back into the side-by-side position, and they shuffle.
- He extends his arms and leads the women toward each other. They pat their free hands.
- He pulls the women back into the side-by-side position, and they shuffle.

Pattycake (1). *Start like this. The man holds the women's hands, and they shuffle shoulder to shoulder. Each woman may hold up the hem of her skirt or keep her free hand behind her back.*

Pattycake (2). *He pulls the women out in front, where they bounce off one another's hands, then pulls them back to his side. Do it two or three times.*

139

Spin. *Pull the ladies out in front at an angle to you. Raise your hands above your head and rotate your palms, thumbs down. Ladies, look at each other as you come around, so that one is not spinning faster than the other. Two or three turns is adequate.*

(2) Spin
- The man is in the middle, with the women on both sides.
- He raises both hands. The women spin to the outside, two or three times. (The woman on the right spins right; the woman on his left spins left.) Whenever they turn inward, they pause briefly to spot each other, coordinating their turns.
- To stop the spinning, he lowers his hands.

(3) Weave
- The man is in the middle, with the women on both sides.
- He extends his left hand and pulls with his right hand, while the woman at his right ducks under his left arm. He follows her under his left arm.
- Next he extends his right hand and pulls with his left hand, while the woman at his left ducks under his right arm. He follows her under his right arm.
- They repeat these two moves several times.
- To stop the weave, he pulls the women back into the side-by-side position.

Weave (1). *Men, you have to make a decision now—be very decisive. Ladies, if he doesn't make a decision, you might butt heads.*

Weave (2). *Men, pull them one after the other, first the right, then the left.*

Weave (3). *Men, stand in one spot, turning from side to side, while the women weave.*

Weave (4). *The man pulls one in close and holds the other at arm's length. The women circle in different directions, first a small circle, ducking under his arm, then a large circle.*

Weave (5). *Ladies, you have to keep moving. Walk all the way around. Men, after a few turns lower your hands and pull them to your side.*

(4) Sweetheart

• All join hands. The man pulls the women into the center, all touch hands briefly, and they step back at arm's length.

• He raises his left hand and wraps the woman on his left into the sweetheart position on his right. She is in the middle.
• Shoulder to shoulder, they shuffle back and forward.
• He raises his left hand and unwraps the center woman in a right turn. They step back at arm's length.

• He pulls the women into the center, all touch hands briefly, and they step back at arm's length.

• He raises his right hand and wraps the woman on his right into the sweetheart position on his left. She is in the middle.
• Shoulder to shoulder, they shuffle back and forward.
• He raises his right hand and unwraps the center woman in a left turn. They step back at arm's length.

• He pulls the women into the center, all touch hands briefly, and they step back at arm's length.

Sweetheart (1). *Men, tell them to join hands. Fall back at arm's length. Again you have to make a decision. Look at the partner on your left. Raise your left hand, palm out, and fold her into your right side in the sweetheart position.*

Sweetheart (2). *Make sure you're shoulder to shoulder. Shuffle back and then forward, back and forward. As you go forward, unfold her and fall back at arm's length.*

Sweetheart (3). *Then look at the partner on your right. Raise your right hand, palm out, and fold her into your left side in the sweetheart position. Shuffle back and then forward. As you go forward, unfold her and fall back at arm's length.*

Sweetheart (4). *Now it's your turn, men. Raise your right hand and turn to the left. Wrap yourself in the center, between the two women.*

Sweetheart (5). *Shoulder to shoulder, shuffle back a few steps, then forward. Then you unfold.*

- He raises his right arm, turns left, and wraps himself into the sweetheart position, between the two women.
- Shoulder to shoulder, they shuffle back and forward.
- He raises his right arm and unwraps himself in a right turn. They step back at arm's length.

- He pulls the women into the center, all touch hands briefly, and they step back at arm's length.

(5) Pinwheel
- All hold hands.
- The women raise their hands across from him, and he ducks under them and turns left. With all hands in the center, all face left and shuffle counterclockwise. (If the man calls "change," reversing direction they face right and shuffle clockwise.)
- After a few shuffles, he bends and backs out. They step back at arm's length.

- He pulls the women into the center, all touch hands briefly, and they step back at arm's length.

- The pinwheel move is repeated with each woman in turn.

- At the end, he pulls the women into the center, all touch hands briefly, and they fall back.

Pinwheel (1). *The man usually starts the pinwheel. Then it's the turn of the woman on his left. She ducks and starts under the raised hands opposite her and turns left.*

Pinwheel (2). *Emerging from under the hands, she turns slightly left and places her right hand behind her back. All hands should be close together in the center.*

Pinwheel (3). *All three whirl to the left, counterclockwise. After a turn or two, pull the hand of the woman on your left, and she backs out. Then all fall back into a circle. The other woman then ducks under.*

(6) Window

- All hold hands.
- He releases the women's hands, reaches across, and takes their other hands in front of him. The women take one another's hands above his forearms.
- He raises both hands, bending his elbows and bringing his forearms together. The women turn away from him, one turn to the outside. (The woman on the right turns right, the woman on the left turns left.) Keeping his hands raised, he lowers his elbows to shoulder height. This forms two little windows, through which the women look at each other.
- They shuffle back and forward.
- To release, he raises both hands. The women turn away from him, to the inside. (The woman on the right turns left, the woman on the left turns right.)
- All release hands and then take up hands in a circle.

- He pulls the women into the center, all touch hands briefly, and they step back at arm's length.

Window (1). *Men, drop the women's hands, reach across, and take their joined hands.*

Window (2). *Ladies, when he drops your hand, reach across and hold each other's hand.*

Window (3). *Ladies, when he raises both hands, turn away from him one turn to the outside.*

Window (4). *And you lower your hands to form two little windows.*

Window (5). *Look at each other as you shuffle back and forth.*

(7) Swing

- All hold hands.
- He drops his right hand and swings each woman in turn while the other woman circles him, as follows:
- As he ducks under the women's raised hands, he holds the waist of the woman on his left and takes her through a left turn, until he meets the woman on his right.
- Then he holds the waist of the woman on his right and takes her through a right turn, until he meets the woman on his left.
- When she is not being turned by him, each woman circles him in the opposite direction. While the women, holding hands, continue to circle him, he swings one after the other, turning left and right on the same spot.
- To release, after swinging either woman, he straightens and takes both their hands. They step back at arm's length.

- He pulls the women into the center, all touch hands briefly, and they step back at arm's length.

Swing (1). *Men, start by dropping your right hand. Bending slightly, hold the waist of the woman on your left and duck beneath their raised hands.*

Swing (2). *You take her through a left turn. Meanwhile, the other woman circles the turning pair.*

Swing (3). *Then you hold the waist of the lady on your right and take her through a right turn.*

Swing (4). *You alternately take the waist of one lady after the other, swinging them in opposite directions.*

Two-Couple Routine

Two couples dance: first man and woman, second man and woman. The first man leads them through several moves, calling out each move and giving directions. (Here we list seven moves, not necessarily danced in the order given.) They dance the shuffle to a two-step tune.

(1) Side-by-Side
- They line up side by side, from left, second man and woman, first man and woman, all facing forward. Holding hands with elbows bent, in the side-by-side position, they shuffle forward and back.
- To release, they step apart and hold hands in a circle. (The first man first calls, "Join hands.")

- The first man pulls the others into the center, all touch hands briefly, and they step back at arm's length.

Side-by-Side. *From their left, second man and woman, first man and woman. Shuffle forward and back.*

(2) Sweetheart Exchange

- All hold hands in a circle.
- The first man raises both hands and turns both women to the inside. (The woman on his right turns right, the woman on his left turns left.) They wrap into the sides of the second man in the sweetheart position. As the first man pushes and pulls, all shuffle back and forward.

- The first man, telling each woman what to do, pulls both women to his side in the sweetheart position, and all shuffle back and forward. (The woman on his right turns left, the women on his left turns right.)
- Then he alternately pushes and pushes one or both women, as they go back and forth to the second man's side. He times the move with the flow of the shuffle back and forward.

Sweetheart Exchange (1). *To start, all hold hands in a circle.*

Sweetheart Exchange (2). *The first man raises both hands and turns both women to the inside.*

Sweetheart Exchange (3). *Both women wrap into the sides of the second man in the sweetheart position.*

Sweetheart Exchange (4). *The first man gives one or both women a slight push or pull to make them come to him or return to the second man.*

- To release, he places both women in the sweetheart position alongside the second man. He raises both hands, and the two women unfold into a circle.
- The first man pulls the others into the center, all touch hands briefly, and they step back at arm's length.

(3) Duck and Turn
- All hold hands in a circle.
- The first man and woman bend and duck under the second man and woman's raised hands. They emerge and turn to the outside, raising their joined hands. The second man and woman, turning inward (the man turns right, the woman turns left), bend and duck backwards under the first man and woman's raised hands. All end in a circle.
- Next the second man and woman bend and duck under the first man and woman's raised hands. The first man and woman, turning inward (the man turns right, the woman turns left), bend and duck backwards under the second man and woman's raised hands. All end in a circle.

- The first man pulls the others into the center, all touch hands briefly, and they step back at arm's length.

Duck and Turn (1). *Still holding hands, the first couple bends and ducks under the second couple's raised hands.*

Duck and Turn (2). *They emerge and turn to the outside, raising their joined hands. The second couple follow backwards.*

Duck and Turn (3). *The second couple bend and duck backwards under the first couple's raised hands, still holding hands.*

Duck and Turn (4). *The second couple straighten up, and all hold hands in a circle.*

(4) Side-by-Side Turn
- All hold hands in a circle.
- The first man raises both hands and turns the two women around (and they drop both men's hands), so that they are back to back. (The woman on his right turns right; the woman on his left turns left.) All hold hands again, the women facing out, the men in.
- Each man turns right ¼, pulling his partner to his left side. All four are in a straight line side by side, with the two couples facing in opposite directions. (The men are on the outside, the women on the inside.) All shuffle forward in a counterclockwise turn.

- To reverse, each man turns left ½, pulling the opposite woman to his right side. All four are in a straight line side by side, with the two new couples facing in opposite directions. (The men are on the outside, the women on the inside.) All shuffle forward in a clockwise turn.

- To release, the first man turns right, pulling the four apart, and turns the two women around (and they drop both men's hands), so that all are facing the center. (The woman on his right turns right; the woman on his left turns left.) All hold hands and face inward.

- The first man pulls the others into the center, all touch hands briefly, and they step back at arm's length.

Side-by-Side Turn (1). *The first man turns the two women to the outside.*

Side-by-Side Turn (2). *The two women now face out, all catching hands.*

Side-by-Side Turn (3). *The two men turn slightly right, drawing the two women into a row. All turn counterclockwise.*

Side-by-Side Turn (4). *To reverse, the two men turn around to the left, drawing the two women into a row.*

Side-by-Side Turn (5). *All turn clockwise. Get in a straight row, women on the inside, men on the outside.*

Side-by-Side Turn (6). *Men, while turning hold your outside hand across your chest. Hold your inside hand against the other side of the woman's waist.*

(5) Weave
- All hold hands in a circle.
- Dropping each other's hand, the first couple bend and duck under the second couple's raised arms. Holding their corner's waist, the first couple turn to the outside and meet again to take each other's hand. (A *corner* is the woman on the man's left or the man on the woman's right.)

- The first man pulls the others into the center, all touch hands briefly, and they step back at arm's length.

- Dropping each other's hand, the second couple bend and duck under the first couple's raised arms. Holding their corner's waist, the second couple turn to the outside and meet again to take each other's hand.

- The first man pulls the others into the center, all touch hands briefly, and they step back at arm's length.

Weave (1). *The first couple bend and duck under the second couple's raised hands. As they duck, they hold hands together with forearms raised.*

Weave (2). *As they pass under the raised arms, they release each other's hands and take the waist of their corner, turning to the outside.*

Weave (3). *Completing a circle, they meet each other and take hands again.*

Weave (4). *Then they raise hands, and the second couple bend and start through.*

Weave (5). *The second couple emerge and circle with their corner. After a few weaves, the first man draws all into a circle.*

(6) Sweethearts Side by Side
- All hold hands in a circle.
- Each man raises his left hand and turns his corner into the sweetheart position against his right side. He holds his partner's left hand behind his corner's back. The four dancers, in a straight line, move forward in a clockwise turn.

- To release, each man raises his left hand and unwinds his corner. They step back at arm's length.

- Next each man raises his right hand and turns his partner into the sweetheart position against his left side. He holds his corner's right hand behind his partner's back. The four dancers, in a straight line, move forward in a counterclockwise turn.

- To release, each man raises his right hand and unwinds his partner. They step back at arm's length.

- The first man pulls the others into the center, all touch hands briefly, and they step back at arm's length.

Sweethearts Side by Side (1). *Each man raises his left hand and turns his corner into the sweetheart position.*

Sweethearts Side by Side (2). *All four are in a straight row, men on the outside, women on the inside, turning clockwise.*

Sweethearts Side by Side (3). *The men unwrap their corners.*

Sweethearts Side by Side (4). *And all fall back in a circle.*

Sweethearts Side by Side (5). *Each man raises his right hand and turns his partner into the sweetheart position.*

Sweethearts Side by Side (6). *All four are in a straight row, men on the outside, women on the inside, turning counterclockwise.*

(7) Reverse Side-by-Side
- All hold hands in a circle.
- The first man raises both hands and pulls both women toward him, turning each to the outside. (The woman on his right turns left; the woman on his left turns right.) As he lowers hands, all three come together in the reverse side-by-side position, with forearms raised and touching, facing the second man.
- The four dancers shuffle forward and back.
- The first man raises both hands and unwinds the two women to the inside. (The woman on his right turns right; the woman on his left turns left.)

- The first man pulls the others into the center, all touch hands briefly, and they step back at arm's length.

- The second man raises both hands and pulls both women toward him, turning each to the outside. (The woman on his right turns left; the woman on his left turns right.) As he lowers hands, all three come together in the reverse side-by-side position, with forearms raised and touching, facing the first man.
- The four dancers shuffle forward and back.

Reverse Side-by-Side (1). *The first man raises both hands and turns both ladies to the outside.*

Reverse Side-by-Side (2). *He pulls both ladies against him in the reverse side-by-side position.*

Reverse Side-by-Side (3). *They shuffle side by side with the second man still holding the ladies' other hands behind their backs.*

Reverse Side-by-Side (4). *To reverse, the first man unwraps the ladies.*

Reverse Side-by-Side (5). *And the second man raises both hands and turns them to the outside.*

Reverse Side-by-Side (6). *He pulls both ladies against him in the reverse side-by-side position. They shuffle side by side with the first man still holding the ladies' other hands behind their backs.*

Reverse Side-by-Side (7). *He unwraps the women, and all fall back in a circle.*

- The second man raises both hands and unwinds the two women to the inside. (The woman on his right turns right; the woman on his left turns left.)

- The first man pulls the others into the center, all touch hands briefly, and they step back.

Appendix A: Dance Halls, Restaurants, and Honky-Tonks

The following information about places to dance in south Louisiana and east Texas was gathered in the summer and fall of 1992 from numerous sources, especially Macon Fry and Julie Posner's *Cajun Country Guide* (Pelican Publishing Co., 1992), word of mouth, and most of all, the places themselves. The list includes dance halls, restaurants, honky-tonks, lounges, and clubs with Cajun or zydeco dances. We have tried to be accurate, but establishments come and go and schedules change.

Abbeville

Levy's Place, Lafitte Rd. (from La. 14 bypass [Veterans Memorial Dr.], turn north on La. 338 [Lafitte Rd.], 2.5 miles on right). Zydeco dance at least once a month. Way out in the country. (318) 893-7834.

Ponderosa Lounge, 811 Nugier Ave. (La. 14 bypass, turn south between Sonic and Taco Bell into Alphonse Rd., first left into Nugier and 2 blocks). Zydeco dance Sat. 9:30–1. Rough and tumble urban hall, older crowd. (318) 893-2376.

Au Large (east of Breaux Bridge)

Caffery's Alexander Ranch, I-10 exit 109, south to Bridge Rd., left 1.4 miles to Doyle Melançon Rd. (La. 347), right 1.7 miles to Zin-Zin Rd., left 2 miles, ranch on left at corner of Latiolais Loop Rd. Zydeco dance Sat. 10–2 once or twice a month. Outdoor screened pavilion with no sign. (318) 332-5415 or 228-7701.

Dipsy Doodle, 1/4 mile south of Caffery's Alexander Ranch on Zin-Zin Rd. (green building). Zydeco dance on weekends, irregular schedule. Green corrugated steel barn with no sign. (318) 332-4786.

Basile

D.I.'s Cajun Restaurant, La. 97 (9.5 miles south of US 190, or 14 miles north of I-10 exit 65). Cajun band Tue. 7–10 (Nonc Allie), Fri.–Sat. 7:30–10:30. Children invited on bandstand to play spoons and *'tit fer* with musicians. (318) 432-5141.

Ivy's Lounge, La. 97, south of US 190. Cajun dance, irregular schedule. Old wood hall and bar. (318) 432-5800.

Baton Rouge

Brunet's Cajun Restaurant, 135 S. Flannery Rd. (I-12 exit north on O'Neal Lane and 1½ miles to Florida Blvd., then left and west 1½ miles to Flannery). Cajun band Wed. 7:30–10, Sat. 8–11. (504) 272-6226.

Fraternal Order of Police Hall, 10777 Greenwell Springs Rd. Occasional Cajun dance Sat. night. (504) 275-1684.

KC Hall, 11277 Airline Hwy. (corner Sherwood). CFMA dance Fri. 8–11, free dance lessons 7. $3 cover. (504) 293-1558.

Mulate's, 8322 Bluebonnet Rd. (I-10 exit Bluebonnet and go east 2 miles). Restaurant with Cajun band Sun.–Thu. 7:30–10, Fri.–Sat. 7:30–11, Sun. lunch 12:30–2:30. Regular bands: Sun. (Déjà Vu), Mon. (Basin Brothers), Tue. (Cajun Gumbo), Wed. (Breaux Bridge Playboys), Thu. (Cajun Born), Fri. (Rice and Gravy), Sat. (Breaux Bridge Playboys), Sun. lunch (Bill Grass and Kristi Guillory). (504) 767-4794.

Port Allen Community Center, 749 N. Jefferson, Port Allen. Rented by groups in East Baton Rouge Parish with occasional Cajun dance Sat.–Sun. (504) 336-2423.

Ric Seeling's Club-Dance, 2327 Elwick Dr. Dance studio with classes Wed. 7 (beginner), 8 (intermediate), 9 (advanced). Occasional Cajun dance Sat. night. (504) 273-3090.

Varsity, 3557 Highland Rd. (corner Chimes, near LSU campus). Occasional Cajun band Sat. night. (504) 383-0187.

Berwick

Richard's Restaurant, La. 182, Bayou Vista (Berwick, across Atchafalaya River from Morgan City). Cajun band Sun. 3–7 (Cajun Red Hots). $1 cover. (504) 395-9575 or 395-7282.

Breaux Bridge

Club Delight, La. 94 behind Expressline food store. Zydeco dance Fri.–Sat. 10–2, Sun. 8–12. (318) 234-9645 or 232-1372.

Harry's Club, 519 Parkway Dr. (I-10 exit 109 and south 2 blocks, then left on Parkway). Cajun dance 1st Sat. 9–1 (Joe Douglas) and occasional Sun. 5–9. Regular Sun. bands: Sheryl Cormier, Johnny Sonnier, Richard LeBoeuf. Large dance floor, older crowd, weddings, and CFMA meetings. $2.50 cover. (318) 332-5180.

Kaiser's Place, La. 94 (½ mile west of Mulate's). Cajun dance Fri. 8:30–12:30, Sun. 6–10, jam session Sat. 3–7. Old-time dance hall, wood frame honky-tonk. $2 cover. (318) 332-1167.

Mulate's, 325 Mills Ave. (I-10 exit 109 to La. 94 and west 1 mile). Large restaurant with Cajun band Mon.–Wed. 7:30–10, Thu.–Sun. 7:30–10:30, Sat. lunch 12–2, Sun. lunch 12–2:30. Regular bands: Sun. (Steve Riley & Mamou Playboys), Mon.–Tue. (Breaux Bridge Playboys), Thu. (Steve Riley & Mamou Playboys), Fri. (Cajun Tradition), Sat. (Dixie Ramblers), Sat.–Sun. lunch (Breaux Bridge Playboys). (318) 332-4648, (800) 634-9880 in La. or (800) 422-2586 in U.S.

La Poussière, 1301 Grand Point Rd. (La. 347 east). Cajun dance Sat. 8:30–12:30 (Walter Mouton & Scott Playboys). Old-time dance hall, large floor, older crowd. $2 cover. (318) 332-1721 or 228-2733.

Sugar Mill Seafood Patio, 282 Rees St. Cajun or zydeco band Fri.–Sat.–Sun. 9 till. (318) 332-4120 or (800) 487-5820.

Butte La Rose (south of Henderson)

Frenchmen's Wilderness Campground, I-10 exit 121, south .7 miles to mall, campground on right. Cajun dance Sat. 8–12 for campers and others. Free. (318) 228-2616.

Cade (south of Lafayette)

Podnuh's, La. 96. Mainly country and swamp pop, but Cajun or zydeco some weekends. Large dance floor, older crowd. (318) 394-9082.

Carencro

La Boucanière Acadienne, 3601 N. University Ave. (2nd red light on University off of I-49). Cajun dance Fri.–Sat. 9–1, Sun. 7–11. (318) 896-0539.

Préjean's, 3480 US 167 (I-49), north Carencro (I-10 exit 103B north 2 miles north, exit 3 to service road, on right just before Evangeline Downs). Restaurant with Cajun band Sun.–Thu. 7–9, Fri. 7:30–10, Sat. 7–11. Regular bands: Woody Daigle, Mamou, Gervais Matte, Blackie Forestier. (318) 896-3247.

Cecilia (north of Breaux Bridge)

Davis Lounge, La. 31 (1 mile south of Friendly Lounge). Zydeco dance, irregular schedule. Old-time dance hall. No phone.

Friendly Lounge, La. 31 (north from Breaux Bridge). Zydeco dance about twice a month in rickety old hall. (318) 667-8543.

Church Point

Le Vieux Presbytère, 837 E. Ebey. Old-time *bal de maison* every other Sat.

7–10. Ladies in Cajun attire (long dress and *garde-soleil*), dance lessons for children, food and drink. (318) 684-2739 or 684-5435.

Crowley

Bélizaire's Cajun Restaurant, 2307 N. Parkerson Ave. (I-10 exit 80 and 1 block south on La. 13). Cajun band Thu. 8–10, Fri.–Sat. 8–11, Sun. 4–8. Regular bands: Nonc Allie (every Sun.), Les Amis (every other Thu.), Waterhole Jammers (every other Thu.), Walter Mouton & Scott Playboys, Jambalaya, Sheryl Cormier, Richard LeBoeuf, Lee Benoit, Jason Fry. Large dance floor. (318) 788-2501.

Crown Point

Bayou Barn, La. 45 at La. 3134 (road from New Orleans to Lafitte). Cajun dance Sun. 12–6 (often Treater). $3 cover. (504) 689-2663.

Delcambre

Smiley's Bon Ami, La. 14 on way to Erath. Cajun dance Sun. 6–10. Formerly The Red Carpet or Carpet Room. No phone.

Duson (west of Lafayette)

Harold's Lounge, 104 Third St. Cajun dance Sat. 8–12 (Bill Pellerin or Woody Daigle). (318) 873-8932.

Elton

Lurcy's Cajun Family Restaurant, US 190 in center of town, 18 miles west of Eunice. Cajun jam session Mon. 7–10, Fri. 7–11. Regular band: usually Rogers Raiders, but anyone may play. (318) 584-5168.

Erath

Smiley's Bayou Club, La. 14 in center of town. Cajun-country dance Sat. 9–1, Cajun dance Sun. 2–6, Cajun jam session Fri. 7:30 till. Large dance floor, older crowd. $3 for men to dance (waitress staples red ticket on your collar). No phone.

The Wild Wild West, La. 339 just north of La. 14. Cajun dance Sun. 6–10. Small dance hall and bar. (318) 937-4325.

Eunice

Dup's Lounge (Carrière's), about 4 miles north of town on La. 13 (road to Mamou). Cajun dance Sat. 11:30 A.M. till (Joe Fontenot and Carl Thibodeaux). Old bar, big dance floor sprinkled with cornmeal. (318) 457-9162 or 457-7576.

Gilton's Club, US 190 3 miles east of town at intersection of La. 95, 1 block south (sign points to club). Zydeco dance Sat. once a month 9–1 (Boozoo Chavis and other popular bands). Huge roadhouse (more than 1,500 seats), largest dance floor in south Louisiana (2,200 square feet), seafood. (318) 457-1241 (recorded message, leave reservation).

Homer's, 555 E. Laurel. Cajun dance Fri. 8–12. (318) 457-5922.

Lakeview Club, about 4 miles north of town on La. 13, in Allen's Lakeview Park (just past Dup's). Cajun dance Sat. 8–12 (Felton LeJeune and Black Mouton). Large dance floor, older crowd. Free for campers, $1 others. (318) 546-0502.

Liberty Theater, S. Second St. and Park Ave. "Rendez Vous des Cajuns" radio broadcast of Cajun and zydeco bands (and comedians and cooks) Sat. 6–8 (KJJB Eunice 105.5 FM, KEUN Eunice 1490 AM, KRVS Lafayette 88.7 FM). Dance floor at foot of stage. Admission $2. (318) 457-7389 or 457-6575.

VFW Restaurant and Dance Hall, E. Laurel (US 190). Cajun dance Sat. night. (318) 457-1055.

Hayes

Harris's Restaurant, La. 14 in Hayes. Cajun band Wed. 7–10 (Eric Oblanc), Fri. 7–11. Older crowd. (318) 622-3582.

Henderson

Angelle's Atchafalaya Basin Bar, Levee Rd. Cajun dance two weekends a month. (318) 228-8567 or 667-6135.

McGee's Atchafalaya Café, 1339 Levee Rd. (I-10 exit 115 south, left on La. 352, then right at Levee Road). Cajun band Fri.–Sat. 8–10, Sun. 1–3, 4–8. (318) 228-7555.

Houma

A-Bear's Restaurant, 809 Bayou Black Dr. (US 90 and La. 311). Cajun band Fri. 6:30–10 (Black and Sondra Guidry), and anyone may play or sing. No dance floor, but customers sometimes dance between tables. (504) 872-6306.

Gino's, 3019 Grand Caillou Rd. (La. 57, just past Houma airport). Cajun dance Fri. 8:30–12:30 (Cajun Moon), free dance lessons Wed. 7–9, CFMA dance 1st Tue. 8–10. (504) 876-4896.

Houston, Texas

Pe-Te Cajun BBQ House and Dance Hall, 11902 Galveston Rd. (I-45 south, exit 30 across Ellington Field). Zydeco dance Sat. 2–6, Cajun dance 3rd Sat. 8–12. Radio broadcast Sat. 6–9 A.M. (KPFT 90.1 FM). (713) 481-8736.

Jennings

Cajun Country Club, La. 26 north (1 mile north of I-10, Elton-Jennings exit). Cajun-country dance Fri.–Sat. 9–1, Cajun dance Sun. 4–8. (318) 824-9113.

Lafayette

Acadian Village, 200 Green Leaf Dr., south of Lafayette (I-10 exit 100 and Ambassador Caffery Pkwy. south to signs on right). Restored bayou town, open daily 10–5. Cajun band on special occasions. Entrance fee. (318) 981-2364 or (800) 962-9133.

Acadiana's Catfish Shak & Cajun Dance Hall, 5818 Johnston St. Cajun dance Fri.–Sat. 7:30–10, Sun. 5:30–8:30. (318) 988-2200, fax 988-4543.

"Downtown Alive!" street dance in 600 block of Jefferson (downtown) Fri. 5:30–8 April–June and Sept.–Nov. Cajun, zydeco, and other bands, different each week. Large crowds. (318) 268-5566.

El Sid O's Zydeco & Blues Club (Sid O's, Sid's), 1523 N. St. Antoine (I-10 exit 103A south about 1 mile, right on Willow, then right on St. Antoine, club at corner Martin Luther King Dr.). Zydeco dance Fri.–Sat. 7–2, Sun. 6–12. Regular bands: Nathan and the Zydeco Cha Chas, Rockin' Sidney, John Delafose, Lynn August, Zydeco Force. New hall, big dance floor. $5 cover. (318) 237-1959 or 235-0647.

Gayon's Zydeco, 1919 Breaux Bridge Hwy. (La. 94), behind gas and grocery. Zydeco dance usually two weekends a month. (318) 237-4645.

Grant Street Dance Hall, 113 Grant (I-10 exit 103A south to Jefferson, then right 2 blocks to corner Grant). Cajun or zydeco dance Sat. 9–1 (but sometimes R & B, rock and roll, etc.). Regular bands: Zachary Richard, Rockin' Dopsie, Mamou. Young crowd. $4 cover. (318) 237-8513.

Hamilton's Place, 1808 Verot School Rd. (I-10 exit 103A south to Pinhook, right 3 miles to Verot School Rd., then right to club on right). Zydeco dance Fri.–Sat. 9–2 two weekends a month. Big old wooden roadhouse. (318) 984-5583.

Maison Creole, 102 N. Washington. Zydeco dance Sat. 9–2. Regular bands: Sampy and the Bad Habits, Fernest Arceneaux and the Thunders. (318) 234-9260.

Randol's Restaurant & Cajun Dance Hall, 2320 Kaliste Saloom Rd., southwest Lafayette (I-10 exit 100, south on Ambassador Caffery

Pkwy. about 5 miles, then left on Kaliste Saloom for restaurant on left). Family restaurant with large *salle de danse*. Cajun band Sun.–Thu. 7–10, Fri.–Sat. 7–11. Regular bands: Jambalaya, Blackie Forestier, The Cajun Tradition. (318) 981-7080 or (800) YO-CAJUN.

Vermilionville, 1600 Surrey St., across from airport (I-10 exit 103A south and Evangeline Thruway through city). Portrayal of bayou settlement. Cajun or zydeco dance in *le Jour de Fête* (performance center) Mon.–Thu. 1–4 (times may vary seasonally), Fri.–Sun. 12–5, occasional special dances. Large dance floor. Admission fee. (318) 233-4077 or (800) 99-BAYOU.

Lake Arthur

VFW Post, Third St. (La. 14 to east side of town and north on Third, 1 mile on right). Cajun dance Sun. 2–6. $2 cover. (318) 774-2946.

Lake Charles

Lloyd's Lounge, 4101 US 90 east (I-10 exit I-210 to US 90, then east). Country-Cajun dance Fri.–Sat. 8:30–12:30. Regular bands: August Broussard, Lon Miller, Dillard Duplaichin. Tiny honky-tonk. (318) 436-9160.

Sugar Bear's, La. 378 just outside Westlake. Cajun dance every other Sat. 9–1 (Calcasieu Cajuns). (318) 497-1597.

Teaser's, 5800 US 90 east. Country-Cajun honky-tonk. (318) 436-9140.

Thibodeaux's Hall, 626 Enterprise Blvd. (I-10 exit Enterprise south, turn left on south side of I-10, hall 1 block down at corner Franklin). Zydeco dance two weekends a month. Unusual old two-story hall, formerly Walker's Hall for 25 years. (318) 433-1190.

VFW Post 2130, 1900 Country Club Rd. (take Ryan St. south from I-210, it becomes University Dr. and then Country Club). Cajun dance Fri.–Sat. 8–12 (Jessie Legé). CFMA meeting and dance 1st Mon. 6. $2.50 cover. (318) 477-9176.

Lawtell (west of Opelousas)

Offshore Lounge, going west from Opelousas on US 190, take second right past Matt's Museum and over railroad tracks to end of dirt road (red barn). Zydeco jam session Thu. 9:30–1:30, dance some weekends. Barbecue and links. (318) 543-9996.

Richard's Club, US 190 just east of Lawtell (4 miles west of Opelousas). Zydeco dance Fri.–Sat. 9:30–1:30, sometimes Sun. 7–1. Big-name bands. Large club with elevated wooden floor. $5 cover. (318) 543-6596.

Leesville

American Legion Post 387, 500 Vernon Rd. (La. 1211 west), Newllano. Cajun dance last Sat. (318) 238-1601.

Lewisburg (south of Opelousas)

Bourque's Club, Cedar St. (south from Opelousas on La. 357 about 8 miles, right at Weston's Grocery on La. 759 for .2 mile, then right .2 mile to pine grove on left). Cajun dance Sat. 9–1, Sun. 6–10. Regular bands: Felton LeJeune, Patrick Thibodeaux, Joe Fontenot. Sat. $3 single, $5 couple, Sun. free. (318) 948-9904 or 948-8646.

Guidry's Friendly Lounge, just before Bourque's. Cajun dance Sun. 5–9 (Passe Partout or Bill Pellerin). Old-time dance. No cover. (318) 942-9988 or 942-6929.

Loreauville (north of New Iberia)

Clifton's Club, Croche Lane (enter town on La. 86, just past Patio Restaurant go west on La. 3242 1.3 mile, left on Landry Rd. 2 miles, then left on Croche Lane [parish road 409] 1 mile, club on left). Zydeco dance every other month or so. Huge dance hall owned by late Clifton Chenier, now by his widow, Margaret. (318) 229-6036 or 367-9912.

Mamou

Diana's Brass Rail, 416 Sixth St. (two doors from Fred's). Cajun band Sat. afternoon 12:30–4:30 (J. C. Labbie) following Fred's Lounge program. (318) 468-4100.

Fred's Lounge, 420 Sixth St. (corner Chestnut), downtown Mamou. Cajun band Sat. morning 9–1 (Donald Thibodeaux & Musical Cajuns) with radio broadcast in French 9–11 (KVPI Ville Platte 1450 AM). Small bar in business since 1946, crowded with local people and tourists. (318) 468-5411 or 468-5234.

Papa Paul's, corner Poinciana (La. 1160) and Second, north edge of town. Zydeco dance Fri.–Sat. 9–2. Rising young stars. Regular bands: Miss Ann Goodly and the Zydeco Brothers, Jo Jo Reed and the Happy Hill Gang, Zydeco Blazers. Elevated wooden floor. (318) 468-5538.

Mandeville

Thibodeaux's Music Hall, 1623 Montgomery St. Cajun dance Wed. 7–11. $3 cover. (504) 626-1616.

New Orleans area

American Legion Hall, 3001 River Rd. (at Causeway), Jefferson. CFMA meeting and dance 1st Mon. 7. (504) 467-9016.

Cajun Cabin, 501 Bourbon (Vieux Carré). Cajun band daily 7–12, Fri.–Sun. 4–1. Regular bands: Sat.–Mon. (Allen Fontenot & Country Cajuns), Tue.–Fri. (Can't Hardly Playboys). Small dance floor. (504) 529-4256.

Cajun Catfish House, 521 Central Ave., Jefferson. Cajun band Sat. 9–1, Sun. 6–10. (504) 733-9944.

Chalet Lounge, 3201 Houma Blvd., Metairie. Cajun band Thu. 9–1 (Terry Bonnette & Bayou Self). (504) 455-2989.

Check Point Charlie's, 501 Esplanade Ave. Cajun band Mon. 9–2. (504) 947-0979.

Chez Tasso, Holiday Inn, 2929 Williams Blvd., Kenner (east bank). Cajun band Fri. 6–10 (Pierre Descant & Cajun Fiddler Band), buffet and free dance lessons. (504) 467-5611.

Dutch Alley, 900 block of Decatur (Vieux Carré). Outdoor tent with large dance floor. Cajun or zydeco dance Sun. 12–3 several times a year. Sponsored by Jean Lafitte National Park or French Market Corp. (504) 589-3718 or 522-2621.

Firemen's Hall, 307 Fourth St., Westwego. Cajun dance usually Sun. afternoon, sometimes other days. (504) 341-8264 or 899-0615.

Four Columns, 3711 Westbank Expwy., Harvey. Cajun dance Tue. 7:30–11 (often Waylon Thibodeaux), dance lessons 6:30. Free food, door prizes, raffle. (504) 340-4109 or 340-8203.

Kristal Seafood Cajun Café, Millhouse at 600 Decatur (Vieux Carré). Cajun band Sat. 1–10, Sun. 1–5 (Don Duet). Small dance floor. (504) 522-0336.

Maple Leaf Bar, 8316 Oak St. (Carrollton area). Cajun dance Thu. 10:30–2:30 (Filé), zydeco dance Fri. 10:30–2:30 (Rockin' Dopsie). Small dance floor. $4–5 cover. (504) 866-9359 or 866-LEAF.

Michaul's Live Cajun Music Restaurant, 701 Magazine (corner Girod). Restaurant with Cajun band nightly except Sunday and Catholic holidays, Mon.–Thu. 7–11, Fri.–Sat. 7:30–12, free dance lessons 6:30 weekdays and 7 weekends. Regular bands: La Touché, Don Duet, Mamou. Large dance floor. (504) 522-5517.

Mulate's, 201 Julia (across from Riverwalk and Convention Center). Large restaurant with Cajun band every night 7:30–11, Sun. 1. Regular bands: Sun. (various), Mon. (Rodney Miller), Tue. (Basin Brothers), Wed. (Bruce Daigrepont), Thu. (Breaux Bridge Playboys), Fri. (Steve Riley & Mamou Playboys), Sat. (Cajun Tradition), Sun. lunch (Trahan, Reed & Vidrine). (504) 522-1492 or (800) 634-9880.

Storyville Comedy and Music, 1104 Decatur (Vieux Carré). Zydeco band occasional Sat. midnight. (504) 522-2500.

Tipitina's, 501 Napoleon Ave. (corner Tchoupitoulas). Famous music club with Cajun dance Sun. 5–9 (Bruce Daigrepont). Large dance floor. $4 cover. (504) 895-3943.

Opelousas

Slim's Y Ki Ki, north end of town on US 167 (left side, across from Piggly Wiggly's). Zydeco dance every other Fri. and every Sat. 9:30–1:30, Sun. if next day is holiday. Big-name bands such as Boozoo Chavis, Zydeco Force. $5 cover. Big old hall, dark and sprawling with low ceiling, air-conditioned. (318) 942-9980, reservations (318) 942-6242 or 948-6649.

Toby's Little Lodge, 1 mile south of town on La. 182 (3.5 miles south of US 190). Cajun dance Thu. 8–11. Lounge next to restaurant with same name. (318) 948-7787.

Parks (south of Breaux Bridge)

Double D Cotton Club (Dauphine's Tuxedo Club), take La. 31 south from Breaux Bridge 5 miles, left and cross Bayou Teche on La. 350, right on La. 347 .3 miles, left on St. Louis Rd. (at green church) to end of road. Zydeco dance Sat. 10–2 most weeks. Regular bands: Nathan and the Zydeco Cha Chas, John Pugh, Russell Garden, Buckwheat Zydeco. (318) 394-9616 or 845-4880.

Port Arthur, Texas

Fish Net Restaurant, 2600 Memorial Blvd. (take I-10 exit south on Tex. 69, almost to Tex. 87). Cajun band Wed. 6–9. Small dance floor. (409) 983-3731.

Rodair Club, Tex. 365. Cajun dance Sat. 8:30–1, Sun. 3–7. Regular bands: Rodney LeJeune and Jessie Legé, Robert Matthews & Bayou Beat Band, Sheryl Cormier, Blaine Thibodeaux & French Ramblers, Jerry Bellot & Cajun Friends. Large dance floor. $3 cover. (409) 736-9001 or 736-1721.

Raceland

Lions Club, end of Hospital Dr. off La. 1 in south Raceland. Occasional Cajun dances, Wed. night lessons. (504) 537-9266.

St. Martinville

Tee's Connection, 704 S. Main. Zydeco dance every other Sat. 9 or 10 till.

Regular bands: Nathan and the Zydeco Cha Chas, Buckwheat Zydeco, C. J. Chenier. (318) 394-3870.

Scott (west of Lafayette)

Triangle Club, La. 93, St. Mary's St. in Scott, west of Lafayette (I-10 exit 97). Cajun dance Fri.–Sat. 9–1, Sun. 5–9. Usual bands: Fri. (James Savoy), Sat. (Johnny Sonnier), Sun. (Percy Boudreaux). Jam session 1st Sat. of month. Large dance floor. $2 cover. (318) 234-0724.

Sulphur

VFW Post 8107, 1325 E. Napoleon. Cajun dance Sat. 9–1. (318) 527-9517.

Sunset

The China Ball, La. 93 south out of Sunset, right on La 356 to dead end at parish 2-40 (club on left). Zydeco dance, irregular hours. Old dance hall in existence since about 1930. No phone.

Thibodaux

Howard Johnson Hotel, La. 308 at Canal Blvd. Cajun dance Sat. morning 9–12 (Cajun Red Hots), radio broadcast (KTIB Thibodaux 640 AM). (504) 447-9071.

Ville Platte

Snook's Bar, main street in town (US 167). Cajun dance Fri. 3–1, Sat. 8–12 (Donald Thibodeaux & Musical Cajuns), Sun. 5–9 (Donald Thibodeaux & Musical Cajuns) with radio broadcast 5–7 (KVPI Ville Platte 1050 AM). Large dance floor with seating for 250, open since 1946. (318) 363-0451.

Acadiana has several business outlets important to Cajun music and dancing. Two of them are:

Savoy's Music Center, east of Eunice on US 190. Owned by accordion-maker and musician Marc Savoy. Cajun jam session every Sat. morning 9–12, musicians welcome. (318) 457-8490 or 457-7389.

Floyd's Record Shop, 434 E. Main St., Ville Platte (US 167 one-way going south). Open Mon.–Fri. 8–6 and Sat. 8–5. Excellent selection of Cajun and zydeco records, tapes, and CDs. Floyd Soileau also owns Swallow Records, a leading recorder of Cajun and zydeco music. (318) 363-2139.

Appendix B: Fairs, Festivals, and Special Events

For precise information on dates and locations, see the annual edition of *Louisiana Celebrations: Fairs, Festivals, and Events,* published by the Louisiana Office of Tourism, P.O. Box 94291, Dept. 383, Baton Rouge, LA 70804-9291, (504) 342-8119 ext. 383. The quarterly magazine *Acadiana Profile* also publishes an annual tour and festival guide, P.O. Box 52247, Lafayette, LA 70505, (318) 235-7919. Major festivals with dancing are indicated by a star (*).

January

La Boucherie du Vermilionville, Vermilionville, 1600 Surrey St., Lafayette, last Sunday. (318) 233-4077 or (800) 99-BAYOU.

Cajun Music Festival of New Orleans, Firemen's Hall, 307 Fourth St., Westwego, third Sunday. (504) 899-0615.

Le Jour de Roi, Vermilionville, 1600 Surrey St., Lafayette, Sunday after Jan. 6. (318) 233-4077 or (800) 99-BAYOU.

Louisiana Fur and Wildlife Festival, building behind courthouse, off Smith St., Cameron, second weekend. (318) 775-5718 or 775-5784.

Newcomer Cajun Bands Festival, Vermilionville, 1600 Surrey St., Lafayette, second weekend. (318) 233-4077 or (800) 99-BAYOU.

February

Louisiana Boudin Festival, Arceneaux Park, between La. 182 and US 90, Broussard, third Sunday before Mardi Gras. (318) 837-9541 or 346-1958.

February and March (Carnival)

Acadian Village Courir du Mardi Gras, Acadian Village, 200 Greenleaf Dr., Lafayette, Saturday before Mardi Gras, starts 9:30 with courir at 4:30. Cajun, zydeco, swamp pop bands. (318) 981-2364 or (800) 962-9133.

Basile Mardi Gras, Railroad Ave. and countryside, Basile. Courir for children on Sunday before Mardi Gras, for men and women on Mardi Gras. (318) 432-5569.

Cajun Mardi Gras Fest, Bayou Barn, La 45 and 3135, Crown Point, Lundi Gras (day before Mardi Gras). (504) 689-2663.

Carencro Mardi Gras, Sunday before Mardi Gras. Parade at 1, bands and food following. (318) 232-6714.

CFMA Chapitre de Lafayette Annual Mardi Gras Dance, Lafayette, Saturday or eve of Mardi Gras. (318) 232-7819.

*Church Point Courir du Mardi Gras, Sunday before Mardi Gras. Courir starts at 9, music, food, dancing all day at Saddle Tramp Riding Club, parade down Main St. at 2, riders perform Mardi Gras march at 3. (318) 684-5693 or (800) 346-1958.

Le Courir du Mardi Gras, Saddle Tramp Riding Club, 1031 E. Ebey St., Church Point, Sunday after Mardi Gras. (318) 684-5186 or 684-2026.

Elton Mardi Gras Run, Elton and countryside, on Mardi Gras. (318) 584-2218 or 584-2570.

*Eunice Courir du Mardi Gras, downtown Eunice and countryside, on Mardi Gras, all day. Family celebration with courir, parade, costume contest, Cajun bands, food. Adults may participate in courir for a fee. (318) 457-6575 or (800) 346-1958.

Eunice Mardi Gras Dance, St. Thomas More Church, Eunice, Saturday before Mardi Gras at 8. (318) 457-7389 or 457-6540.

Grand Marais Mardi Gras, College Rd., off US 90 east, Jeanerette, on Mardi Gras at 11. Parade, bands, dancing, food. (318) 276-4713.

La Grande Boucherie des Cajuns, city park, N. Main St., St. Martinville, Sunday before Mardi Gras. (318) 394-6819 or 346-1958.

Jennings Mardi Gras, Main St., Jennings, Saturday before Mardi Gras. (318) 821-5500.

Krewe of Chic-à-la-Pie Parade, Kaplan. Parade on Mardi Gras at 2, street dance following parade. (318) 643-8402.

Loreauville Mardi Gras, Main St., Loreauville, on Mardi Gras at 1. Parade, bands, dancing, food. (318) 229-6825.

*Mamou Mardi Gras, downtown Mamou and countryside, on Mardi Gras 8 A.M.–midnight. Big and rowdy with courir, processions, Cajun bands, dance at American Legion Hall. (318) 468-3272 or (800) 346-1958.

*Mardi Gras in Cajun Country, downtown Lafayette, Saturday through Mardi Gras. (318) 232-3808 or (800) 346-1958.

Prairie Cajun Mardi Gras, Vermilionville, 1600 Surrey St., Lafayette, third Sunday before Mardi Gras. Re-enactment of rural Mardi Gras celebration, music, dancing, food. (318) 233-4077 or (800) 99-BAYOU.

'Tit Mamou-Iota Mardi Gras Folklife Festival, on Mardi Gras. Courir for women only in 'Tit Mamou 7–3, festival in downtown Iota 9–5. Cajun food, music, dancing, crafts. (318) 779-2456.

Vermilionville Community Mardi Gras, Vermilionville, 1600 Surrey St., Lafayette, Sunday before Mardi Gras. (318) 233-4077 or (800) 99-BAYOU.

Many towns and cities in Acadiana have parades and balls with Cajun bands and dancing.

March

Boggy Bayou Festival, La. 1172, Pine Prairie, second full weekend. (318) 599-2031.

Cajun Fun Fest, Catholic High School, 1301 De La Salle Dr., New Iberia, second weekend. Cajun music and food. (318) 364-5116.

City Park Spring Festival, City Park, New Orleans, third weekend. (504) 482-4888.

Earth Fest, Audubon Park, New Orleans, third weekend. (504) 861-2537.

Festival du Courtableau, Main St., Washington, fourth weekend. (318) 826-3627 or 826-3072.

Iowa Rabbit Festival, Iowa, third weekend. (318) 582-7176 or 582-6120.

Ragin' Cajun Spring Fest, Cajun Field, corner W. Congress St. and Bertrand Dr., Lafayette, fourth weekend. (318) 231-5392 or (800) 346-1958.

Taste of the Bayou Country Food Festival, Holiday Inn Holidome, 210 S. Hollywood Rd., Houma, first Sunday. (504) 868-2732.

World Championship Crawfish Etouffée Cook-Off, Northwest Pavilion, Samuel Dr., Eunice, last Sunday. (318) 457-2565 or (800) 346-1958.

April

Acadiana Charter Chapter CFMA Music Festival, Eunice, first Sunday. (318) 457-4709.

L'Anniversaire de Vermilionville, 1600 Surrey St., Lafayette, first weekend. (318) 233-4077 or (800) 99-BAYOU.

Blessing of the Shrimp Fleet, Broussard's Canal, La. 56, Chauvin, third Sunday. (504) 594-5859.

Cajun Day, Port Allen, fourth Sunday. (504) 647-7092.

Cajun Food and Fun Festival, Our Lady of Seven Dolors Church, Adam St., Welsh, fourth weekend. (318) 734-4772.

Carbon Black Festival, Willow St. behind St. Mary Parish courthouse, Franklin, weekend nearest April 26 every even-numbered year. Street dancing. (318) 828-3853.

Congé, Academy of the Sacred Heart, off Church St., Grand Coteau, a Sunday usually in April. (318) 662-5494.

Creole Festival, Holy Rosary Church, 1900 E. Main St., Houma, first weekend after Easter Day. (504) 876-7652.

Creole Festival on the Teche, City Park, Wormser St., Jeanerette, fourth weekend. (318) 276-3615.

Festival de la Prairie, St. John the Evangelist Church, 15208 La. 73, Prairieville, fourth weekend. (504) 673-8307.

*Festival International de Louisiane, downtown Lafayette, six days in third week. (318) 232-8086 or (800) 346-1958.

French-Acadian Music Festival, Knights of Columbus Hall, 102 W. Vermilion St., Abbeville, second Saturday after Easter. (318) 893-1257.

Golden Triangle CFMA Chapter Festival, Rodair Club grounds, Tex. 365, Port Arthur, Texas, last weekend. (409) 866-3104.

Gonzales Strawberry Festival, 421 E. City Park St., Gonzales, second to last weekend. (504) 644-1978.

Jam-Bal-Aya du Musique, Acadian Village, 200 Greenleaf Dr., Lafayette, first weekend. Louisiana music, with *bal de maison* Saturday. (318) 232-3797.

Le Jour de Cajun, Kaplan Recreation Center, La. 14, corner Mill and Saltzman sts., Kaplan, third weekend. (318) 643-2190.

Laurel Valley Heritage Festival and Family Reunion, La. 308 south of Thibodaux, fourth Sunday. (504) 447-7456 or 447-2902.

Loreauville Firemen's Festival, Loreauville, second weekend. (318) 229-6825.

Louisiana Railroad Days Festival, Railroad Museum Park, La. 27, Lake Charles Ave., DeQuincy, second weekend. (318) 786-7115.

*New Orleans Jazz and Heritage Festival, Fair Grounds, New Orleans, two weekends at end of April and early May. Cajun and zydeco bands play on raised stands with large open spaces for dancing. (504) 522-4786.

Ponchatoula Strawberry Festival, Ponchatoula, second weekend. (504) 386-8349.

St. Bernard Crawfish Festival, Meraux, first weekend. (504) 277-9552.

Shriever Firemen's Festival, St. Bridget's Church, Shriever (La. 24 between Thibodaux and Houma), third weekend unless Easter. (504) 447-7962.

May

Allons Danser! Vermilionville Cajun Dance Contest, Vermilionville, 1600 Surrey St., Lafayette, last weekend. (318) 233-4077 or (800) 99-BAYOU.

Bayou Barn Boogie, La. 45 and 3135, Crown Point, fourth Sunday. (504) 689-2663.

*Breaux Bridge Crawfish Festival, Parc Hardy, Breaux Bridge, first full weekend. (318) 332-6655 or (800) 246-1958.

Cajun Fais Do-Do, St. Joseph's Church, Thibodaux, third Sunday. (504) 446-6652.

Cajun Heartland State Fair, Cajundome, 444 Cajundome Blvd., Lafayette, ten days near beginning of month. (318) 265-2100 or (800) 346-1958.

Carlyss Cajun Bon-Ton Festival, Sulphur, third weekend. (318) 583-4800.

Central Catholic School Fair, Morgan City, last weekend. (504) 385-5372.

Cochon de Lait, downtown, off La. 1, Mansura, first full weekend. (318) 253-4551 or 964-5286.

*Contraband Days, Lake Charles Civic Center, 900 Lakeshore Dr., Lake Charles, first two weeks. (318) 436-5508.

Fais Do-Do, Naval Air Station, Belle Chasse, third Sunday. (504) 393-3260.

Fest for All, Baton Rouge, third weekend. (504) 335-3378.

Le Festival du Poisson Armé (Garfish Festival), Sacred Heart Church, 154 Cypremort Rd., Baldwin, first full weekend. (318) 923-7781 or 923-4603 or (800) 256-2931.

Festival sur la Teche, downtown, Teche Dr. on bayou side, Franklin, fourth weekend. (318) 828-6322 or 828-0779 or (880) 256-2931.

Holy Rosary Family Fun Fest, Holy Rosary Church, 415 E. Main St., Larose, first full weekend. (504) 693-3342.

Lake Arthur Extravaganza and Beach Party, Lake Arthur Park, 101 Arthur Ave., Lake Arthur, third weekend. (318) 774-2211.

Louisiana Praline Festival, St. Gregory Church, 439 Sixth St., Houma, first weekend. (504) 872-2384 or 868-3725.

New Orleans CFMA Chapter Annual Music Festival, Mudbug's, Gretna, third Sunday. (504) 392-0202.

Sacred Heart Fun Fest, municipal auditorium, US 90 and Myrtle St., Morgan City, second weekend. (504) 384-8108.

*St. Landry Parish Heritage Festival, courthouse square in Opelousas, city hall and Liberty Theater in Eunice, Old Washington High School grounds in Washington, and various parts of Sunset and Grand Coteau, first weekend. (318) 942-2683 or (800) 424-5442 or (800) 346-1958.

Sorrento Crawfish Festival, Ascension Civic Center, Reynolds Lambert Park, US 61, Sorrento, third weekend. (504) 675-8515.

Spring Food Fest, Holy Saviour School, 201 Church St., Lockport, third weekend. (504) 532-2536.

*Spring Zydeco Festival, Lake Martin Rd. east of Lafayette, second Sunday (Mother's Day). Sponsored by KJCB in Lafayette (770 AM). (318) 233-4262.

*Thibodaux Firemen's Fair, fairgrounds, Tiger Dr., Thibodaux, first full weekend. (504) 447-6197 or 447-1986.

*Zydeco Extravaganza, Blackham Coliseum, 2330 Johnston St., Lafayette, last Sunday. (318) 234-9695 or (800) 346-1958.

June

Bayou Lacombe Crab Festival, Lacombe Park, Hwy 190, Lacombe, fourth weekend. (504) 882-5528.

Bayou Indian Festival, city park, Henderson St. and St. Paul St., off US 90, Elton, third weekend. (318) 584-2653.

Bon Mangé Festival, Vacherie-Gheens Community Center, La 654, Gheens, first weekend. (504) 532-8219.

Cajun Country Festival, Raceland, third weekend. (504) 468-4516 or 447-3610.

*Church Point Buggy Festival, Church Point City Park, Lougaree St., Church Point, first weekend. Street dance. (318) 684-2739 or (800) 346-1958.

*Festival des Cadiens, Firemen's Hall, 307 Fourth St., Westwego, fourth Sunday. (504) 899-0615.

Festival des Vieux Temps, Vermilionville, 1600 Surrey St., Lafayette, fourth weekend. (318) 233-4077 or (800) 99-BAYOU.

Galliano Cajun Festival, behind St. Joseph's Church, Galliano, third weekend. (504) 475-6785.

Great French Market Tomato Festival, New Orleans, first weekend. (504) 522-2621.

Jambalaya Festival, downtown Gonzales, second weekend. Street dancing. (504) 647-3601.

Lake Arthur Father's Day Celebration, park, 101 Arthur Ave., Lake Arthur, third Sunday. (318) 774-2211.

*Mamou Cajun Music Festival, Eighth St. and Hackberry St., Mamou, first weekend. Outdoor dancing on wooden platform. (318) 468-3272 or (800) 346-1958.

South Lafourche Cajun Seafood Festival, Golden Meadow and Galliano, third weekend. (504) 448-3652.

Zydeco Bay-Ou, Bayou Barn, La. 45 and 3135, Crown Point, third Sunday. (504) 689-2663.

July

L'Après Midi de Sortière, Vermilionville, 1600 Surrey St., Lafayette, July 4. (318) 233-4077 or (800) 99-BAYOU.

Bastille Day Weekend, Vermilionville, 1600 Surrey St., Lafayette, weekend near July 14. (318) 233-4077 or (800) 99-BAYOU.

Bastille Days, Kaplan Recreation Center, Mill St. and Saltzman St., Kaplan, weekend near July 14. (318) 643-2400.

*Cajun Music and Food Festival, Burton Coliseum, 6400 S. Common St., Lake Charles, third weekend. (318) 583-7511.

Erath Festival, Erath, July 4 weekend. (318) 937-8401.

The Fourth Futurity Festival, Carencro, July 4 weekend. (318) 233-1006.

Hackberry Marshland Festival, Hackberry Multiservice Facility, La. 27, Hackberry, July 4 weekend. Sunday is French music day. (318) 762-3566.

Louisiana Catfish Festival, St. Gertrude Church, La. 631, Des Allemands, weekend after July 4 weekend. (504) 758-7542.

Louisiana Freedom Festival, city park, Elton, July 3–6. (318) 584-2156.

Louisiana Oyster Festival, Cut Off Youth Center (behind Sacred Heart Church), La. 1, Cut Off, third weekend. Dance contest. (504) 632-6990.

*Mulate's Accordion Festival, Mulate's, 325 Mills Ave., Breaux Bridge, first weekend. (318) 332-4648 or (800) 346-1958.

Natchitoches/NSU Folk Festival, Prather Coliseum, College Ave., Natchitoches, third weekend. (318) 357-4332 or 352-8072 or (800) 259-1714.

St. Charles Parish Festival, Norco, fourth Saturday. (504) 764-7166.

Vacherie Independence Day, Vacherie, July 4 weekend. (504) 265-2265.

Many towns have July 4 festivals including Cajun dancing.

August

Alligator Day, Hammond, third Saturday. (504) 345-3617.

Bayou Food Fest, Bayou Barn, La. 45 and 3235, Crown Point, last Sunday. (504) 689-2663.

Blessing of the Fleet Festival, Community Center, La. 1, Grand Isle, third weekend. (504) 787-2385.

Blessing of the Shrimp Fleet, Mobil dock, Cameron, first Saturday. (318) 775-5222.

Bull Club Fair and Blessing of the Fleet, Golden Meadow, second weekend. (504) 475-5428 or 475-7537.

*"Le Cajun" Music Awards and Festival, Blackham Coliseum, 2330 Johnston St., Lafayette, third weekend. (800) 487-0981 or (800) 346-1958.

*Cajun Riviera Festival, beach near waterslide area, Holly Beach, second weekend. Dancing on the beach. (318) 775-5516.

*Delcambre Shrimp Festival, festival grounds, Railroad and Richard sts., Delcambre, third weekend. (318) 685-2653.

Le Festival du Lapin de la Grand Prairie, St. Peter's Church, La. 748 and 363, Grand Prairie, last weekend. (318) 826-3272.

Festival of Riches, New Iberia Recreation Center, City Park, New Iberia, second weekend. Square dancing, round dancing, clogging, and Cajun dancing. (318) 365-7590.

Fête des Acadiens, Acadian Village, 200 Greenleaf Dr., Lafayette, third Saturday. (318) 981-2364 or (800) 962-9133.

Jean Lafitte Seafood Festival, City Park Dr., Lafitte, second weekend. (504) 689-2208.

Lagniappe by the Bayou, White Castle, first weekend. (504) 545-3623.

St. Bonaventure's Rockin' Cajun Festival, Avondale, second weekend. (504) 436-1211.

South Lafourche Seafood Festival, Galliano, second weekend. (504) 632-4633.

Summer Music Festival, Arceneaux Park, La. 182, Broussard, last weekend. (318) 837-FEST or (800) 346-1958.

Summertime Cajun Music Fest, Firemen's Hall, 307 Fourth St., Westwego, last Sunday. (504) 899-0615.

September

Alligator Festival, US 90, Boutte, fourth weekend. (504) 785-2571.

Alligator Harvest Festival, Grand Chenier State Park, La. 82, Grand Chenier, last Sunday. (318) 775-5718.

Ascension Parish Fair, Prairieville, fourth weekend. (504) 673-8245.

Assumption Parish Heritage Festival, Napoleonville, last weekend. (504) 252-9586.

Bal d'Hangar, Acadian Village, 200 Greenleaf Dr., Lafayette, third Saturday. (800) 962-9133.

Bayou Blue Food and Fun Festival, St. Louis Church, 2226 Bayou Blue Rd., Bayou Blue (near Houma), first weekend after Labor Day. (504) 876-3449.

Bon Ton with the Cajuns, St. Ann's Church, 4353 La. 24, Bourg (south of Houma), third weekend. (504) 594-3548.

Les Bon Vieux Temps sur le Chenal (Lakeland Church Fair), La. 414 across from Chenal cemetery, Jarreau. (504) 627-5124.

Cajun Extravaganza, Ascension Civic Center, Sorrento, fourth Sunday. (504) 675-8515.

Cajun Heritage Festival, youth center, La. 1, Cut Off, second weekend. (504) 537-5444.

Cajun Oktoberfest, Holiday Inn Holidome, 210 S. Hollywood Rd., Houma, last Sunday. (504) 879-4288.

*Calca "Chew" Food Festival and Fair, Burton Coliseum, 6400 S. Common St., Lake Charles, second weekend. (318) 439-4585.

A Cultural A-Fair at le Vieux Village, Opelousas, third Sunday. (318) 948-4731.

Dog Hill Labor Day Festival, home of Boozoo Chavis at 115 Petah Rd., Lake Charles, Labor Day. (318) 828-4889.

Festival of Beauties, Youngsville Center (La. 92 east) and elementary school gym, Youngsville, third full weekend. Starts with Friday night *fais do-do.* (318) 856-6238.

*Festivals Acadiens, seven festivals at various locations in Lafayette, third weekend. *Downtown Alive!* street dance in 600 block of Jefferson St. on Fri. 5:30–8. *Festival de Musique Acadienne* in Girard Park on Sat.–Sun. 11–7:30 with many Cajun (and a few zydeco) bands, outdoor dancing. No admission fee. (318) 232-3737 or 232-3808 or (800) 346-1958.

La Fête Bateau Lafitte, St. Anthony's Church, La. 45, Lafitte, fourth weekend. (504) 689-4101.

La Fête du Bayou, youth center, La. 1, Cut Off, fourth weekend. (504) 632-7616.

Franklin Cajun Fest, Teche Dr. behind courthouse, Franklin, Labor Day weekend. (318) 828-6303 or (800) 346-1958.

Jeanerette Old Country Fair, city park, Wormser St., Jeanerette, first weekend. (318) 276-4293.

Les Jeux d'Hier (the Games of Yesterday), Vermilionville, 1600 Surrey St., Lafayette, third weekend. (318) 233-4077 or (800) 99-BAYOU.

Louisiana Creole Food Festival, Chalmette, fourth weekend. (504) 271-1664.

*Louisiana Shrimp and Petroleum Festival, downtown Morgan City, Labor Day weekend. Street dance and square dance. (504) 385-0703.

*Louisiana Sugar Cane Festival and Fair, corner Jefferson Terr. and 20 Arpent Rd., New Iberia, last full weekend. (318) 369-9323 or (800) 346-1958.

Makin' Music, Bogue Falaya Park, Covington, fourth weekend. (504) 624-8407 or 522-1635.

Maringouin Labor Day Fair, Maringouin, Labor Day weekend. (504) 625-2333.

New Orleans CFMA Labor Day Music Festival, Firemen's Hall, Westwego, Sunday before Labor Day. (504) 341-8264.

Pirogue Festival, Jim Bowie Park, off US 90, Houma, Labor Day. (504) 868-2732.

*Rayne Frog Festival, Gossen Memorial Park, Frog Festival Dr., Rayne, third weekend. Begins with *fais do-do.* (318) 334-2332 or (800) 346-1958.

St. Andrew Cajun Fest, St. Andrew's Church, 833 Julia St., Amelia, fourth weekend. (504) 631-2333 or (800) 256-2931.

St. Lawrence Catholic Church Bazaar, La. 102, Raymond. (318) 824-3011 or 824-3763.

Southwest Louisiana State Fair and Expo, Lake Charles Civic Center, Lake Charles, fourth weekend. (318) 436-7575.

*Southwest Louisiana Zydeco Music Festival, Southern Development Foundation Farm, Plaisance (parish road 5-75-3 off US 167 between Opelousas and Ville Platte), Saturday before Labor Day. (318) 942-2392.

Vinton Cajun Festival, St. Joseph's Church, 1502 Industrial St., Vinton, third weekend. (318) 589-7358.

October

Andouille Festival, Ormond Plantation, 8407 River Rd., Destrehan, last full weekend. (504) 652-3544 or 764-8544.

*Boucherie Festival, Ascension Civic Center, US 61, Sorrento, second full weekend. (504) 675-5355.

Bridge City Gumbo Festival, Angel Square, 1701 Bridge City Ave., Bridge City, second weekend. (504) 341-3448.

Cajun Heritage and Music Festival, Acadian Village, 200 Greenleaf Dr., Lafayette, second weekend. (318) 984-6110 or (800) 346-1958.

*Calcasieu-Cameron Fair, La. 27 north, Sulphur, full week beginning fourth Monday after Labor Day. (318) 527-9371.

Church Point Cajun Day Festival, Saddle Tramp Club grounds, 1036 E. Ebey St., Church Point, first weekend. (318) 684-2739.

Creole Folklife Weekend, Vermilionville, 1600 Surrey St., Lafayette, second weekend. (318) 233-4077 or (800) 99-BAYOU.

Donaldsonville Sunshine Festival, downtown Donaldsonville and Louisiana Square, first weekend. (504) 473-4727.

Festival under the Oaks, First United Methodist Church, 621 Little Bayou Black Dr., Houma, first Saturday. (504) 868-7787.

French Food Festival, Larose Regional Park, Bayou Lafourche and Intracoastal Canal, Larose, last full weekend. (504) 693-7355.

French Louisiana Heritage Festival, Kenner, fourth weekend. (504) 455-2555.

Full Moon Swamp Excursion and Party, Bayou Barn, La. 45 and 3135, Crown Point, third weekend. (504) 689-2663.

Home Grown Music Festival, park, 101 Arthur Ave., Lake Arthur, third Saturday. (318) 774-2528.

International Acadian Festival, festival park on La. 1, 2 miles south of Plaquemine, third weekend. (504) 687-3359 or 687-4161.

International Alligator Festival, Hanson High School, Anderson St., Franklin, first weekend after close of alligator season. (318) 828-3487.

International Rice Festival, downtown Crowley, third weekend. (318) 783–3067 or (800) 346-1958.

Jeff Fest, Lafrenière Park, Jefferson Parish, third weekend. (504) 888-2900 or 888-3322.

Jefferson Davis Parish Fair, fairgrounds, La 26 south, Jennings, first weekend. (318) 824-1773.

Lafourche Parish Agricultural Fair and Livestock Show, fairgrounds, 99 Texas St., Raceland, second weekend. (504) 446-1316.

*Lagniappe on the Bayou Fair, St. Joseph Church, 5232 La. 56, Chauvin, third weekend. Nightly *fais do-do*. (504) 594-5878 or 594-5859.

Laurel Valley Heritage Festival, La. 308 south of Thibodaux, second Sunday. (504) 446-7456.

Louisiana Cajun and Zydeco Music Festival, Sabra David Dr., off La. 35, Kaplan, second Saturday. (318) 643-7456 or 643-8481 or 643-8860.

Louisiana Cattle Festival, Concord St. and State St., downtown Abbeville, first weekend. (318) 643-2620.

*Louisiana Cotton Festival, Cotton Festival Fairgrounds, La. 3042, 3 miles northeast of Ville Platte, second full week. Includes old-time *contredanse* and *fais do-do*. (318) 363-2193.

Louisiana Gumbo Festival, behind Our Lady of Prompt Succor Church, La. 20, Chackbay, third weekend. (504) 633-7789 or 633-9949 or 633-2828.

*Louisiana Swamp Festival, Audubon Zoo, New Orleans, first and second weekends. Cajun and zydeco bands and dance demonstrations at several places in zoo. Large open space for dancing at Hibernia Pavilion. (504) 861-2537.

*Louisiana Yambilee Festival, Yambilee Fairgrounds, US 190 west, Opelousas, last full weekend. (318) 948-8848 or (800) 346-1958.

October Fête, Maltrait Memorial School, 612 N. Hebert St., Kaplan, third weekend. (318) 643-6472.

Opelousas Catholic School Fair, Opelousas, first weekend. (318) 942-5404.

Our Lady of the Lake Family Fun Festival, Lake Arthur Christian Unity Center, E. Eighth St., Lake Arthur, second weekend. (318) 774-3175.

Pointe Coupée Parish Fair, Scott Memorial Civic Center and False River Park, New Roads, usually third weekend. (504) 638-9858 or 638-8825.

Rapides Parish Fair, Rapides Coliseum on La. 28 west, Alexandria, third weekend. (318) 473-6605.

St. Philomena Cajun Country Festival, St. Philomena School, 110 Convent St., Labadieville, first weekend. (504) 526-8508.

*Sauce Piquante Festival, St. Mary Nativity Church, La. 1 north, Raceland, first full weekend. (504) 537-6682 or 537-7544.

Terrebonne Livestock and Agricultural Fair and Rodeo, Houma Air Base, La. 24 south, Houma, first weekend. (504) 594-7178.

Vermilion Fair and Festival, Kaplan Recreation Center, corner Mill and Saltzman sts., Kaplan, second weekend. (318) 643-2400.

La Vie Lafourchaise, St. Hilary's School, 306 Twin Oaks Dr., Mathews (below Raceland), third weekend. (504) 537-3546.

West Baton Rouge Potpourri Festival, citywide, Port Allen, second weekend. (504) 336-2426.

November

Abbeville French Market Festival, Magdalen Square, downtown Abbeville, first weekend. (318) 893-2491 or (800) 346-1958.

Broussard Community Fair, St. Cecilia School, Main St., Broussard, weekend before Thanksgiving. (318) 837-1864.

Calcasieu Cajun Festival, Cal-Cam Fairgrounds, 1109 Cypress St., Sulphur, first full weekend. (318) 527-5261.

CFMA Bayou Extravaganza, youth center behind Sacred Heart Church, La. 1, Cut Off, second Saturday. (504) 632-7616.

Christmas on the Teche, Bouligney Plaza, Main St., New Iberia, last weekend. (318) 365-NIJC.

Country/Cajun Thanksgiving Fair, Bayou Barn, La. 45 and 3135, Crown Point, last Sunday. (504) 689-2663.

Destrehan Plantation Annual Fall Festival, Destrehan Plantation, 9999 River Rd., Destrehan, second weekend. (504) 764-9315.

Fall Cajun Music Fest, Firemen's Hall, 307 Fourth St., Westwego, second Sunday. (504) 899-0615.

Festival à la Campagne, Picard Park, Milton, second weekend. (318) 893-7082.

Le Festival Dulac, Central Catholic High School, Morgan City, second weekend.

Gueydan Duck Festival, Gueydan Duck Festival Park, La. 14, Gueydan, second weekend. (318) 536-6780 or (800) 346-1958.

Harvest Fest, Loreauville, fourth weekend. (318) 229-6363.

*Louisiana Folklife Festival, in front of the Liberty Theater, S. Second St. and Park Ave., Eunice, second full weekend. (318) 457-6575 or (800) 346-1958.

Louisiana Mountain Music Fest, Pelican Park, US 190, Mandeville (across from Fountainebleau State Park), last weekend. Admission fee. (504) 893-1379.

*Louisiana Swine Festival, Basile Town Park, W. Stagg Ave., Basile, first weekend. (318) 432-6321 or 432-6728 or 432-5437.

La Noce Acadienne, Vermilionville, 1600 Surrey St., Lafayette. (318) 233-4077 or (800) 99-BAYOU.

Noël Acadien au Village, Acadian Village, 200 Greenleaf Dr., Lafayette, last weekend and first two weekends in December. (318) 984-6110.

Pelican Festival, Mamou, first Saturday. (318) 468-5139.

Port Barre Cracklin Festival, Saizan St. across from city hall, off US 190, Port Barre, second weekend. (318) 585-6251.

Terre Historical and Cultural Society Fall Market Days, Southdown Plantation near Houma, second weekend. (504) 873-8832.

December

A Bayou Christmas, South Lafourche High School, La. 308, Galliano, second weekend. (504) 632-8900.

Bayou Christmas Festival, Bayou Barn, La. 45 and 3135, Crown Point, Sunday before Christmas. (504) 689-2663.

Cajun Country Christmas, 120 S. Irma Rd., Gonzales, first Friday. (504) 647-2841.

Christmas in Old Opelousas, Opelousas, second week. (318) 948-4731.

Festival of the Bonfires, Lutcher and Gramercy, third weekend. (504) 869-8623.

Oak Alley Plantation Christmas Bonfire Party, Oak Alley Plantation, river road on west bank above Vacherie, second Saturday. (504) 265-2151.

Plaquemines Parish Fair and Orange Festival, Fort Jackson, first weekend. (504) 564-2951.

Appendix C: Calls for Circle Dances

The following simple calls are derived partly from Marie del Norte Thériot and Catherine Brookshire Blanchet's *Les Danses Rondes: Louisiana French Folk Dances* (Abbeville, La., 1955) and partly from quadrilles. In the old *danses rondes*, there were no calls, and rural, largely illiterate dancers performed the steps from memory while singing children's songs. In an attempt to describe the steps, Thériot and Blanchet used many of the calls of *Les Lanciers* and other quadrilles, which originated in New Orleans but spread to Cajun areas of Louisiana.

Today groups may wish to perform circle dances to waltzes and two-steps, as well as to the old songs. Unless the dancers rehearse the moves, and can perform them smoothly, we suggest that leaders use the following calls. This method is similar to that used in quadrilles and American square dances.

All form a circle of partners, women to right of men, with any number of dancers. One of the dancers (or someone else) calls the moves in English or French. Start with salute and circle right, then go through all the moves, especially those in which the dancers change partners, and repeat them as needed. Most moves last 4 or 8 measures.

Allemande left (allemande gauche)
Corners join left arms, with hands holding each other's elbows, turn each other once around, and return to place.

Allemande right (allemande droite)
Partners step forward and pass each other by the left shoulder. They meet new partners, join right arms, with hands holding each other's elbows, turn each other once around, and return to place.

Balance (balancez)
Partners (or corners) face each other. They step left, bringing the right foot together. Then they step right, bringing the left foot together. (Often followed by swing.)

Circle right (tournez à droite)
All join hands and circle to the right. Depending on the rhythm, they shuffle the two-step or the waltz. At the start of the dance, the circle always moves to the right; later it may move left (tournez à gauche).

Dishrag (la lavette)
Partners join both hands and turn around, man right and woman left, ending face to face.

Do-si-do (dos à dos)
Partners face each other, pass each other by the right shoulder, circle each other back to back, and return to place.

Forward and back (en avant et en arrière)
Hands joined, all take four steps to the center and four steps back to place.

Grand right and left (la chaîne des dames)
Partners face each other and join right hands. They pass each other and take the left hand of the next dancer. Men move right and women left, alternately taking right and left hands as they move around the circle. (The caller may ask the dancers to link elbows instead of clasping hands.)

The figure may last until all have rejoined their partners, halfway around the circle. Partners then promenade right to their original place.

If the figure lasts only 4 or 8 measures, each man keeps as a new partner the woman whose hand he holds at the end of the figure.

Grand right and left past four partners
In a more elaborate version, each man goes completely around the fourth woman, holding left hands and turning left, and does the grand right and left back past two women, keeping the third as a new partner. (His original partner is to his left.)

Make an arch (faites un arc)
All join hands. The lead couple (caller and partner) or any other couple turn left, sideways to the circle, and make an arch with their hands. The man drops the hand of the woman to his left. She ducks under the arch, and all the rest follow.

Promenade (promenez)
Side by side and facing right, partners cross hands (left over right) and move counterclockwise around the ring.

The caller may direct all to change partners. At the end of the promenade, the man moves up to the woman ahead.

Salute (saluez)
Partners honor each other. The man bows slightly, and the woman curtseys. It is also customary to salute one's corner, the dancer on the other side of you.

Sashay (chassez croisé)

All face the center of the circle. Sliding sideways, men move right and behind women, while women move left and in front of men. They return to place the opposite way.

Swing (un tour de mains)

Partners (or corners) turn clockwise, shuffling in time with the music. They use one of three methods to hold each other:

1. Link right elbows.

2. Join both hands, facing each other and keeping elbows close to the body (the method used in old circle dances and quadrilles).

3. Hold each other in the waltz position, but almost side to side with right sides touching (the method used in American square dances).

The caller may direct all to swing and change partners. Partners swing one and a half times around, ending with the woman to the left in the circle. Both face the center. The man takes the woman to his right as a new partner.